Employers Liability Claims: A Practical Guide Post-Jackson

Andrew Mckie,
Barrister at Law, Clerksroom (Manchester),
LLB Hons, PG DIP and
Former Solicitor Advocate,
Personal Injury, Fraud, Credit Hire

Law Brief Publishing

Published 2016 by
Law Brief Publishing
30 The Parks
Minehead
Somerset
TA24 8BT

www.lawbriefpublishing.com

Paperback: ISBN 978-0-9575530-8-8

PREFACE

Since 2013 Employers' Liability Claims have seen dramatic changes. Practitioners have seen the introduction of the Low Value Portal, The Enterprise and Regulatory Reform Act 2013, and Fixed Costs for claims that exit the Low Value Portal.

All these changes have impacted the ability of Personal Injury Solicitors to Act for sometimes severely injured Claimants involved in accidents in the workplace. Personal Injury Solicitors have an important role in holding insurers to account in workplace claims and allowing Access to Justice. It may be argued therefore, that this type of litigation has become much less attractive to personal injury law firms, and the introduction of fixed recoverable costs raises real questions about access to justice.

This book therefore looks at all aspects of the claims process for low value personal injury Employers' Liability Claims from inception of the claim through to Trial.

The aim of this book is to provide a clear but comprehensive guide to this area of practice, that can be utilised by practitioners on a day-to-day basis, in Claimant and Defendant practice.

The book has a focus on running an Employers' Liability Claim, in an efficient way post Jackson, spotting the winners and vetting the losing claims early on.

I would encourage the reader to 'dip in and out' of the book as and when required.

I wish to thank Tim Kevan of Law Brief publishing for providing me with the opportunity to write this book and the PI Brief Update website for publishing relevant sections.

Andrew Mckie
Personal Injury Barrister
January 2016

Contents

CHAPTER ONE
THE PORTALS AND FIXED PORTAL COSTS IN EL CLAIMS

The Low Value Portals in Employers' Liability Claims came into effect for any claim where the accident date is on or after 31 July 2013. The purpose of this chapter is to examine the most important aspects of the Portals in the context of Low Value Personal Injury claims, for claims that start off with the Low Value Portal but then exit the Portal.

The Portals can be found at:-
http://www.justice.gov.uk/courts/procedure-rules/civil/protocol/pre-action-protocol-for-low-value-personal-injury-employers-liability-and-public-liability-claims#2.1

Which types of claims does the Portal apply to?

Paragraph 4.1 of the Portal helpfully sets out which claims they apply to:-

4.1 *This Protocol applies where—*
(1) either—
(a) the claim arises from an accident occurring on or after 31 July 2013; or
(b) in a disease claim, no letter of claim has been sent to the defendant before 31 July 2013;
(2) the claim includes damages in respect of personal injury;
(3) the claimant values the claim at not more than £25,000 on a full liability basis including pecuniary losses but excluding interest ('the upper limit'); and
(4) if proceedings were started the small claims track would not be the normal track for that claim.

It is important to note that if the claim is valued at more than £25,000 on a full liability basis, the claim will not commence in the Low Value Portal. It is also helpful to note that the Protocol ceases to apply to a claim where, at any stage, the claimant notifies the defendant that the claim has now been revalued at more than the upper limit. Some Solicitors make the mistake of thinking that the Low Value Portal applies to accidents before 31 July 2013, and it is important to note it does not, and any accidents before this date, will still attract costs on the standard basis.

Claims to which the Low Value Portal does not apply

There are a large number of scenarios where the Low Value Portal will not apply, and these are set out as follows:-

> *4.3 This Protocol does not apply to a claim—*
> *(1) where the claimant or defendant acts as personal representative of a deceased person;*
> *(2) where the claimant or defendant is a protected party as defined in rule 21.1(2);*
> *(3) in the case of a public liability claim, where the defendant is an individual ('individual' does not include a defendant who is sued in their business capacity or in their capacity as an office holder);*
> *(4) where the claimant is bankrupt;*
> *(5) where the defendant is insolvent and there is no identifiable insurer;*
> *(6) in the case of a disease claim, where there is more than one employer defendant;*
> *(7) for personal injury arising from an accident or alleged breach of duty occurring outside England and Wales;*
> *(8) for damages in relation to harm, abuse or neglect of or by children or vulnerable adults;*
> *(9) which includes a claim for clinical negligence;*
> *(10) for mesothelioma;*
> *(11) for damages arising out of a road traffic accident (as defined in paragraph 1.1(16) of the Pre-Action Protocol for Low Value Personal Injury Claims in Road Traffic Accidents).*

Disease cases fall outside the scope of this book, and will be subject to a separate publication, but it is important to note that mesothelioma cases do not start inside the Low Value Portal, arguably due to their complexity. Additionally, where there is a disease case, with more than one Defendant, such a claim will not start inside the Low Value Portal. Further it may be important to note that the Protocol does not apply, where the Defendant is an individual in the case of a public liability claim, or the defendant is insolvent and there is no identifiable insurer.

The CNF

The Protocol sets out the following stages for completion of the CNF:-

Stage 1
Completion of the Claim Notification Form
6.1
(1) The claimant must complete and send—
(a) the CNF to the defendant's insurer, if known; and
(b) the Defendant Only Claim Notification Form ("Defendant Only CNF") to the defendant,
but the requirement to send the form to the defendant may be ignored in a disease claim where the CNF has been sent to the insurer and the defendant has been dissolved, is insolvent or has ceased to trade.
(2) If—
(a) the insurer's identity is not known; or
(b) the defendant is known not to hold insurance cover,
the CNF must be sent to the defendant's registered office or principal place of business and no Defendant Only CNF is required.
(3) Where the insurer's identity is not known, the claimant must make a reasonable attempt to identify the insurer and, in an employers' liability claim, the claimant must have carried out a database search through the Employers' Liability Tracing Office.
(4) In a disease claim, the CNF should be sent to the insurer identified as the insurer last on risk for the employer for the material period of employment.
6.2 If the CNF or Defendant Only CNF cannot be sent to the defendant via the prescribed Portal address, it must be sent via first class post; and this must be done, in a case where the CNF is sent to the

insurer, at the same time or as soon as practicable after the CNF is sent.

6.3 All boxes in the CNF that are marked as mandatory must be completed before it is sent. The claimant must make a reasonable attempt to complete those boxes that are not marked as mandatory.

6.4 Where the claimant is a child, this must be noted in the relevant section of the CNF.

6.5 The statement of truth in the CNF must be signed either by the claimant or by the claimant's legal representative where the claimant has authorised the legal representative to do so and the legal representative can produce written evidence of that author-isation. Where the claimant is a child the statement of truth may be signed by the parent or guardian. On the electronically completed CNF the person may enter their name in the signature box to satisfy this requirement.

There are a number of significant points that arise from this. Firstly the Claimant Solicitor must ensure that the before the CNF is signed, it is sent to the Claimant to check and the Claimant's Solicitor must have written conformation from the Claimant that the CNF has been agreed. This can be requested by the Defendant's insurer later on in the pro-ceedings. An important part of this process, is that all too often at Trial, the information on the CNF is incorrect, which can affect the credib-ility of the claim at Trial, especially as regards to the mechanism of the accident. Thus, it is essential that the Claimant gets an opportunity to check the CNF before it is submitted to the Defendant's insurer, and the Claimant's Solicitor can make any corrections that are required.

Secondly, sometimes a situation arises where there is no identifiable insurer. The Portal rules require that a search is made of the *Employers' Liability Tracing Office.* The website to undertake the search can be found at:- https://eld.elto.org.uk/TCUsage/TANDC

Thirdly, as with other types of claims, all the mandatory information on the CNF must be completed. There is a warning in the Protocol which sets out:-

Failure to complete the Claim Notification Form
6.7 Where the defendant considers that inadequate mandatory information has been provided in the CNF that shall be a valid reason for the defendant to decide that the claim should no longer continue under this Protocol.

6.8 Rule 45.24(2) sets out the sanctions available to the court where it considers that the claimant provided inadequate information in the CNF.

Exit Points from the Portal

Contributory Negligence, liability not admitted or failure to respond
6.13 The claim will no longer continue under this Protocol where the defendant, within the relevant period in paragraph 6.11 —
(1) makes an admission of liability but alleges contributory negligence;
(2) does not complete and send the CNF response;
(3) does not admit liability; or
(4) notifies the claimant that the defendant considers that—
(a) there is inadequate mandatory information in the CNF; or
(b) if proceedings were issued, the small claims track would be the normal track for that claim.
6.14 Where the defendant does not admit liability the defendant must give brief reasons in the CNF response.
6.15 Where paragraph 6.13 applies the claim will proceed under the relevant Pre-Action Protocol and the CNF will serve as the letter of claim (except where the claim no longer continues under this Protocol because the CNF contained inadequate information). Time will be treated as running under the relevant Pre-Action Protocol from the date the form of acknowledgment is served under paragraph 6.9 or 6.10.

There are therefore a number of ways in which the claim can exit the Portal. It is important for Claimant Solicitors to note the exit points from the Portal and provide appropriate notification to the insurer where an exit point is reached. It is helpful if the Claimant Lawyer has a suitable claims management system that will provide a notification if for example the time limit for investigation expires and there has not been an admission, so the claim can exit the Portal.

Time Limits

> *6.11 The defendant must complete the 'Response' section of the CNF ("the CNF response") and send it to the claimant—*
> *(a) in the case of an employers' liability claim, within 30 days of the step taken pursuant to paragraph 6.1;*

One may therefore often find in practice that given the complexity of these types of cases, the employer and/or their insurer will not be able to realistically investigate the cases within 30 days, and hence the reason for the high drop out rates from the Low Value Portal.

Admissions in the Portal

> *1.1 In this Protocol—*
> *(1) 'admission of liability' means the defendant admits that—*
> *(a) the breach of duty occurred;*
> *(b) the defendant thereby caused some loss to the claimant, the nature and extent of which is not admitted; and*
> *(c) the defendant has no accrued defence to the claim under the Limitation Act 1980;*

It should be noted that if an admission is made, and the Defendant then later exits the Portal, the admission will still be binding, unless the Court's permission is sought to withdraw the admission post-proceedings, or consent is provided. CPR 14.1B says:-

> *Admissions made under the RTA Protocol or the EL/PL Protocol*
> **14.1B**
> *(1) This rule applies to a pre-action admission made in a case to which the Pre-Action Protocol for Low Value Personal Injury Claims in Road Traffic Accidents ('the RTA Protocol') or the Pre-action Protocol for Low Value Personal Injury (Employers' Liability and Public Liability) Claims ('the EL/PL Protocol') applies.*

(2) The defendant may, by giving notice in writing withdraw an admission of causation –

(a) before commencement of proceedings –

(i) during the initial consideration period (or any extension to that period) as defined in the relevant Protocol; or

(ii) at any time if the person to whom the admission was made agrees; or

(b) after commencement of proceedings –

(i) if all the parties to the proceedings consent; or

(ii) with the permission of the court.

(3) The defendant may, by giving notice in writing withdraw any other pre-action admission after commencement of proceedings –

(a) if all the parties to the proceedings consent; or

(b) with the permission of the court.

(4) An application under rule 14.1B(2)(b)(ii) or (3)(b) to withdraw a pre-action admission must be made in accordance with Part 23.

Portal Costs and Disbursements – claims which remain in Portal

Fixed costs in relation to the EL/PL Protocol

Where the value of the claim for damages is not more than £10,000		Where the value of the claim for damages is more than £10,000, but not more than £25,000	
Stage 1 fixed costs	£300	Stage 1 fixed costs	£300
Stage 2 fixed costs	£600	Stage 2 fixed costs	£1300
Stage 3 - Type A fixed costs	£250	Stage 3 - Type A fixed costs	£250
Stage 3 - Type B fixed costs	£250	Stage 3 - Type B fixed costs	£250
Stage 3 - Type C fixed costs	£150	Stage 3 - Type C fixed costs	£150

Fixed costs raise real questions of Access to Justice and how Low Value Claims can be run in a fixed costs environment. Some points to consider are:-

(a) Ensure the correct level of Fee Earner is undertaking the work. There is now little point in Grade A Fee Earners undertaking Low Value cases. The majority of Portal cases now call for Paralegals to undertake the work to make it efficient.

(b) More experienced Fee Earners should be undertaking the higher value and more complex portal cases. However, one has to be cautious to ensure that the Fee Earner undertaking the work has appropriate supervision. One can make the mistake of thinking that dealing with portal work is straightforward. It must be remembered that £25,000 personal injury claims, if litigated, could be in the multi track.

(c) Make sure you have a case management system for Portal Cases. This is particularly useful for exiting claims from the Portal, which often requires the user to exit the claim from the Portal. Proclaim's A2A software is very efficient for Low Value Portal routine cases, and the package of letters includes all the relevant correspondence, which is required when working to very tight fees.

Disbursements in the Portal

45.19
(1) Subject to paragraphs (2A) to (2E), the court –
(a) may allow a claim for a disbursement of a type mentioned in paragraphs (2) or (3); but
(b) will not allow a claim for any other type of disbursement.
(2) In a claim to which either the RTA Protocol or EL/PL Protocol applies, the disbursements referred to in paragraph (1) are –
(a) the cost of obtaining –
(i) medical records;

(ii) a medical report or reports or non-medical expert reports as provided for in the relevant Protocol;

(aa) Driver Vehicle Licensing Authority;

(bb) Motor Insurance Database;

(b) court fees as a result of Part 21 being applicable;

(c) court fees payable where proceedings are started as a result of a limitation period that is about to expire;

(d) court fees in respect of the Stage 3 Procedure; and

(e) any other disbursement that has arisen due to a particular feature of the dispute.

(2A) In a soft tissue injury claim to which the RTA Protocol applies, the only sums (exclusive of VAT) that are recoverable in respect of the cost of obtaining a fixed cost medical report or medical records are as follows—

(a) obtaining the first report from an accredited medical expert selected via the MedCo Portal: £180;

(b) obtaining a further report where justified from an expert from one of the following disciplines—

(i) Consultant Orthopaedic Surgeon (inclusive of a review of medical records where applicable): £420;

(ii) Consultant in Accident and Emergency Medicine: £360;

(iii) General Practitioner registered with the General Medical Council: £180; or

(iv) Physiotherapist registered with the Health and Care Professions Council: £180;

(c) obtaining medical records: no more than £30 plus the direct cost from the holder of the records, and limited to £80 in total for each set of records required. Where relevant records are required from more than one holder of records, the fixed fee applies to each set of records required;

(d) addendum report on medical records (except by Consultant Orthopaedic Surgeon): £50; and

(e) answer to questions under Part 35: £80.

Interim Payments in the Portal

It may be argued that where one had a seriously injured client, for example a serious fracture, where the claim remains in the Portal, the Claimant should always be advised to wait until the end of the prognosis period before settling the claim, to see if he or she recovers in accordance with the prognosis period in the medical report. Many Claimants however, against advice, will often seek to take the money, as they need it because the accident has caused financial hardship. An interim payment can become incredibly useful in such circumstances, whilst the Claimant waits to see how the injuries settle down and to ensure the Claimant is recovered before a claim is settled. The rules set out as follows:-

Request for an interim payment

7.12 Where the claimant requests an interim payment of £1,000, the defendant should make an interim payment to the claimant in accordance with paragraph 7.17.

7.13 The claimant must send to the defendant the Interim Settlement Pack and initial medical reports (including any recommendation that a subsequent medical report is justified) in order to request the interim payment.

7.14 The claimant must also send evidence of pecuniary losses and disbursements. This will assist the defendant in considering whether to make an offer to settle the claim.

7.15 Where an interim payment of more than £1,000 is requested the claimant must specify in the Interim Settlement Pack the amount requested, the heads of damage which are the subject of the request and the reasons for the request.

7.16 Unless the parties agree otherwise—

(a) the interim payment of £1,000 is only in relation to general damages; and

(b) where more than £1,000 is requested by the claimant, the amount in excess of £1,000 is only in relation to pecuniary losses.

Interim payment of £1,000

7.17

(1) Where paragraph 7.12 applies the defendant must pay £1,000 within 10 days of receiving the Interim Settlement Pack.

(2) Sub-paragraph (1) does not apply in a claim in respect of a disease to which the Pneumoconiosis etc. (Workers' Compensation) Act 1979 applies unless there is a valid CRU certificate showing no deduction for recoverable lump sum payments.

Interim payment of more than £1,000

7.18 Subject to paragraphs 7.19 and 7.21, where the claimant has requested an interim payment of more than £1,000 the defendant must pay—

(1) the full amount requested less any deductible amount which is payable to the CRU;

(2) the amount of £1,000; or

(3) some other amount of more than £1,000 but less than the amount requested by the claimant,

within 15 days of receiving the Interim Settlement Pack.

7.19 Where a payment is made under paragraphs 7.18(2) or (3) the defendant must briefly explain in the Interim Settlement Pack why the full amount requested by the claimant is not agreed.

7.20 Where the claim is valued at more than £10,000, the claimant may use the procedure at paragraphs 7.12 to 7.19 to request more than one interim payment.

7.21 Nothing in this Protocol is intended to affect the provisions contained in the Rehabilitation Code.

It should be borne in mind that this process may only be utilised where there is a need for a further report. If the Defendant fails to make the interim payment, the Claimant may exit the claim from the process, subject to the following provisions:-

7.26 Where the defendant does not comply with paragraphs 7.17 or 7.18 the claimant may start proceedings under Part 7 of the CPR and apply to the court for an interim payment in those proceedings.

7.27 Where the defendant does comply with paragraph 7.18(2) or (3) but the claimant is not content with the amount paid, the claimant may still start proceedings. However, the court will order the defendant to pay no more than the Stage 2 fixed costs where the court awards an interim payment of no more than the amount offered by the defendant or the court makes no award.

7.28 Where paragraph 7.26 or 7.27 applies the claimant must give notice to the defendant that the claim will no longer continue under this Protocol. Unless the claimant's notice is sent to the defendant within 10 days after the expiry of the period in paragraphs 7.17, 7.18 or 7.23 as appropriate, the claim will continue under this Protocol.

Fixed Costs and Disbursements – Claims which Exit the Portal

Fixed costs where a claim no longer continues under the EL/PL Protocol – employers' liability claims

A. If Parties reach a settlement prior to the claimant issuing proceedings under Part 7

Agreed damages	At least £1,000, but not more than £5,000	More than £5,000, but not more than £10,000	More than £10,000, but not more than £25,000	
Fixed costs	The total of—(a) £950; and (b) 17.5% of the damages	The total of—(a) £1,855; and (b) 12.5% of damages over £5,000	The total of—(a) £2,500; and (b) 10% of damages over £10,000	

B. If proceedings are issued under Part 7, but the case settles before trial

Stage at which case is settled	On or after the date of issue, but prior to the date of allocation under Part 26	On or after the date of allocation under Part 26, but prior to the date of listing	On or after the date of listing but prior the date of trial	

Fixed costs	The total of— (a) £2,630; and (b) 20% of the damages	The total of— (a) £3,350; and (b) 25% of the damages	The total of— (a) £4,280; and (b) 30% of the damages

C. If the claim is disposed of at trial

Fixed costs	The total of— (a) £4,280; (b) 30% of the damages agreed or awarded; and (c) the relevant trial advocacy fee

D. Trial advocacy fees

Damages agreed or awarded	Not more than £3,000	More than £3,000, but not more than £10,000	More than £10,000, but not more than £15,000	More than £15,000
Trial advocacy fee	£500	£710	£1,070	£1,705

Disbursements for Claims within Fixed Recoverable Costs

45.29I
(1) Subject to paragraphs (2A) to (2E), the court—
(a) may allow a claim for a disbursement of a type mentioned in paragraphs (2) or (3); but
(b) will not allow a claim for any other type of disbursement.
(2) In a claim started under either the RTA Protocol or the EL/PL Protocol, the disbursements referred to in paragraph (1) are—
(a) the cost of obtaining medical records and expert medical reports as provided for in the relevant Protocol;
(b) the cost of any non-medical expert reports as provided for in the relevant Protocol;
(c) the cost of any advice from a specialist solicitor or counsel as provided for in the relevant Protocol;

(d) court fees;

(e) any expert's fee for attending the trial where the court has given permission for the expert to attend;

(f) expenses which a party or witness has reasonably incurred in travelling to and from a hearing or in staying away from home for the purposes of attending a hearing;

(g) a sum not exceeding the amount specified in Practice Direction 45 for any loss of earnings or loss of leave by a party or witness due to attending a hearing or to staying away from home for the purpose of attending a hearing; and

(h) any other disbursement reasonably incurred due to a particular feature of the dispute.

(2A) In a soft tissue injury claim started under the RTA Protocol, the only sums (exclusive of VAT) that are recoverable in respect of the cost of obtaining a fixed cost medical report or medical records are as follows —

(a) obtaining the first report from an accredited medical expert selected via the MedCo Portal: £180;

(b) obtaining a further report where justified from an expert from one of the following disciplines—

(i) Consultant Orthopaedic Surgeon (inclusive of a review of medical records where applicable): £420;

(ii) Consultant in Accident and Emergency Medicine: £360;

(iii) General Practitioner registered with the General Medical Council: £180; or

(iv) Physiotherapist registered with the Health and Care Professions Council: £180;

(c) obtaining medical records: no more than £30 plus the direct cost from the holder of the records, and limited to £80 in total for each set of records required. Where relevant records are required from more than one holder of records, the fixed fee applies to each set of records required;

(d) addendum report on medical records (except by Consultant Orthopaedic Surgeon): £50; and

(e) answer to questions under Part 35: £80.

(2B) Save in exceptional circumstances, no fee may be allowed for the cost of obtaining a report to which paragraph (2A) applies where the medical expert—
(a) has provided treatment to the claimant;
(b) is associated with any person who has provided treatment; or
(c) proposes or recommends treatment that they or an associate then provide.
(2C) The cost of obtaining a further report from an expert not listed in paragraph (2A)(b) is not fixed, but the use of that expert and the cost must be justified.
(2D) Where appropriate, VAT may be recovered in addition to the cost of obtaining a fixed cost medical report or medical records.

What about interlocutory applications?

The costs recovery of interlocutory applications has now become very limited and is set out in CPR 45 as follows:-

Interim applications
45.29H
*(1) Where the court makes an order for costs of an interim application to be paid by one party in a case to which this Section applies, **the order shall be for a sum equivalent to one half of the applicable Type A and Type B costs in Table 6 or 6A.***
(2) Where the party in whose favour the order for costs is made—
(a) lives, works or carries on business in an area set out in Practice Direction 45; and
(b) instructs a legal representative who practises in that area,
the costs will include, in addition to the costs allowable under paragraph (1), an amount equal to 12.5% of those costs.
(3) If an order for costs is made pursuant to this rule, the party in whose favour the order is made is entitled to disbursements in accordance with rule 45.29I.
(4) Where appropriate, VAT may be recovered in addition to the amount of any costs allowable under this rule.

Complex Cases – Amount of Costs Exceeding Fixed Recoverable Costs

There is scope within the rules for a claim for an amount exceeding fixed recoverable costs or predictive costs, where there are 'exceptional circumstances', and it is set out as follows:-

> *Claims for an amount of costs exceeding fixed recoverable costs*
> **45.13**
> *(1) The court will entertain a claim for an amount of costs (excluding any success fee or disbursements) greater than the fixed recoverable costs but only if it considers that there are **exceptional circumstances** making it appropriate to do so.*
> *(2) If the court considers such a claim appropriate, it may –*
> *(a) summarily assess the costs; or*
> *(b) make an order for the costs to be subject to detailed assessment.*
> *(3) If the court does not consider the claim appropriate, it will make an order for fixed recoverable costs (and any permitted disbursements) only.*

There is no current definition in the White Book, as to what this is likely to mean in practice, However, from experience this is likely to potentially apply in the following examples:-

(1) a multi-party claim
(2) a serious injury claim, which for what ever reason is not allocated to the multi track.
(3) Allegations of fraud, with volumes of disclosure.

However, if the application is made and fails, the following consequences will apply:-

> **45.14**
> *(1) This rule applies where –*
> *(a) costs are assessed in accordance with rule 45.13(2); and*

(b) the court assesses the costs (excluding any VAT) as being an amount which is less than 20% greater than the amount of the fixed recoverable costs.

(2) The court must order the defendant to pay to the claimant the lesser of –

(a) the fixed recoverable costs; and

(b) the assessed costs.

Solicitor CFA's Post April 2013

As part of this chapter it is helpful to note the provisions for Conditional Fee Agreements Post April 2013 and success fees from the Claimant post April 2013. They are set out in LASPO 2012 as follows:-

44 Conditional fee agreements: success fees

(4B) The additional conditions are that—

(a) the agreement must provide that the success fee is subject to a maximum limit,

(b) the maximum limit must be expressed as a percentage of the descriptions of damages awarded in the proceedings that are specified in the agreement,

(c) that percentage must not exceed the percentage specified by order made by the Lord Chancellor in relation to the proceedings or calculated in a manner so specified, and

(d) those descriptions of damages may only include descriptions of damages specified by order made by the Lord Chancellor in relation to the proceedings."

This should be read in conjunction with the Conditional Fee Agreements Order 2013, which sets out:-

Specified proceedings

4. A claim for personal injuries shall be proceedings specified for the purpose of section 58(4A)(b) of the Act.

Amount of success fee in specified proceedings

5. (1) In relation to the proceedings specified in article 4, the percentage prescribed for the purposes of section 58(4B)(c) of the Act is —

(a) in proceedings at first instance, 25%; and
(b) in all other proceedings, 100%.
(2) The descriptions of damages specified for the purposes of section 58(4B)(d) of the Act are—
(a) general damages for pain, suffering, and loss of amenity; and
(b) damages for pecuniary loss, other than future pecuniary loss, net of any sums recoverable by the Compensation Recovery Unit of the Department for Work and Pensions.

Thus, in post April 2013 proceedings, the rules suggests that the Solicitor can charge the Claimant 25% of past pecuniary losses and general damages recovered, **but not** future losses and thus the explanatory note sets out in the order:-

Notwithstanding the effect of article 3, section 58(4B) of the 1990 Act, enables the Lord Chancellor, in respect of proceedings specified by order under section 58(4A), to effectively cap the lawyer's success fee at a percentage of specified damages awarded to the client. Article 5 provides that, in a claim for personal injuries, the success fee shall be limited to a maximum of 25% of the damages awarded for pain, suffering and loss of amenity and pecuniary loss, other than future pecuniary loss and net of any sums recoverable by the Compensation Recovery Unit, inclusive of VAT.

Qualified One Way Costs Shifting (QOCS)

Pre-Action Disclosure Applications are not protected by QOCS, nor are proceedings where a claimant has entered into a pre-commencement funding arrangement, which is defined in:-

48.2(1)
A pre-commencement funding arrangement is-

(i)   a funding arrangement as defined by rule 43.2(1)(k)(i) where......"

CPR 43.2(1)(k)(i) defines a funding arrangement as "an arrangement where a person has –

(i)   entered into a conditional fee agreement or a collective conditional fee agreement which provides for a success fee....."

The QOCS rules set out under 44.14:-

Effect of qualified one-way costs shifting

44.14
(1) Subject to rules 44.15 and 44.16, orders for costs made against a claimant may be enforced without the permission of the court but only to the extent that the aggregate amount in money terms of such orders does not exceed the aggregate amount in money terms of any orders for damages and interest made in favour of the claimant.
(2) Orders for costs made against a claimant may only be enforced after the proceedings have been concluded and the costs have been assessed or agreed.
(3) An order for costs which is enforced only to the extent permitted by paragraph (1) shall not be treated as an unsatisfied or outstanding judgment for the purposes of any court record.

Exceptions to qualified one-way costs shifting where permission not required

44.15 *Orders for costs made against the claimant may be enforced to the full extent of such orders without the permission of the court where the proceedings have been struck out on the grounds that –*
(a) the claimant has disclosed no reasonable grounds for bringing the proceedings;
(b) the proceedings are an abuse of the court's process; or
(c) the conduct of –
(i) the claimant; or
(ii) a person acting on the claimant's behalf and with the claimant's knowledge of such conduct,

is likely to obstruct the just disposal of the proceedings.

Exceptions to qualified one-way costs shifting where permission required

44.16
(1) Orders for costs made against the claimant may be enforced to the full extent of such orders with the permission of the court where the claim is found on the balance of probabilities to be fundamentally dishonest.

In order words, if the Claimant proceeds to Trial, and recovers zero, provided that the claim is not found to be fundamentally dishonest, or one of the other exemptions above applies, the Court can still makes a costs order but the Defendant will not be able to enforce it. A County Court Judgment would not be recorded against the Claimant in such circumstances.

The Defendant will in summary, only be able to enforce any order, up to the amount of damages recovered by the Claimant.

QOCS protection may also be lost if the Claimant fails to beat a Defendant's Part 36 offer, but the Defendant will only be able to recover costs up to the level of the Claimant's damages.

QOCS of course took away the need for After the Event insurance cover in relation to Low Value Personal Injury cases in some circumstances, as in effect the Claimant's risk of paying the Defendant's costs has now been taken away except in very limited circumstances.

Claimant Lawyers have to be wary of the rules surrounding fundamental dishonesty. In the case of *Gosling v Screwfix and Anr* (unreported, 29 March 2014) at Cambridge County Court, HHJ Moloney QC ordered the claimant to pay the defendant's costs of the action on an indemnity basis.

The Judge ruled that a Personal Injury Claimant who exaggerated the extent of his ongoing symptoms should be denied the protection of qualified one-way costs shifting (QOCS) on the grounds that the claim was "fundamentally dishonest".

Caution should be expressed in multiple Defendant cases, where it is arguable that QOCS protection may not apply against a Defendant who is sued in a multiple Defendant case, and the case fails against one Defendant. QOCS arguably allows recovery of costs by the Defendant against whom the Claimant has failed, up to the aggregate amount of damages awarded to the Claimant. In such circumstances a *Sanderson* or *Bullock* order should be sought that the compensating Defendant pay the costs order, and the Claimant should take out ATE to cover such a risk.

Defendant's Costs and Part 36 Offers – Post July 2013 Cases

Defendant's Costs can be recovered in certain circumstances within FRC and CPR 45 sets out as follows:-

45.29F

(1) In this rule—

(c) paragraphs (2) to (7) apply to all other cases under this Section in which a defendant's costs are assessed.

(2) If, in any case to which this Section applies, the court makes an order for costs in favour of the defendant—

(a) the court will have regard to; and

(b) the amount of costs order to be paid shall not exceed,

the amount which would have been payable by the defendant if an order for costs had been made in favour of the claimant at the same stage of the proceedings.

(3) For the purpose of assessing the costs payable to the defendant by reference to the fixed costs in Table 6, Table 6A, Table 6B, Table 6C and Table 6D, "value of the claim for damages" and "damages" shall be treated as references to the value of the claim.

(4) For the purposes of paragraph (3), "the value of the claim" is—

(a) the amount specified in the claim form, excluding—
(i) any amount not in dispute;
(ii) in a claim started under the RTA Protocol, any claim for vehicle related damages;
(iii) interest;
(iv) costs; and
(v) any contributory negligence;
(b) if no amount is specified in the claim form, the maximum amount which the claimant reasonably expected to recover according to the statement of value included in the claim form under rule 16.3; or
(c) £25,000, if the claim form states that the claimant cannot reasonably say how much is likely to be recovered.
(6) Where an order for costs is made pursuant to this rule, the defendant is entitled to disbursements in accordance with rule 45.29I
(7) Where appropriate, VAT may be recovered in addition to the amount of any costs allowable under this rule.

Thus for the purpose of the assessment exercise, the Defendant can only recover its fixed costs that would have been payable by the Defendant, to the Claimant, if an order for costs had been made in favour of the Claimant at the same stage in the proceedings.

The Defendant can still of course make Part 36 offers within proceedings to protect its costs position, and the following provisions will apply:-

Where the Claimant accepts an offer after the relevant period has elapsed, or the Defendant achieves judgment more favorable than its offer:

- The Claimant will recover costs calculated based on the stage when the relevant period elapsed and the value of damages recovered

- The Claimant will be liable for the Defendant's costs for the period from the date of expiry of the relevant period to the date of acceptance

- If the parties do not agree the liability for costs then the court will make the determination

- In relation to the defendant's costs the sum awarded by the court "*shall not exceed the fixed costs....applicable at the date of acceptance, less the fixed costs to which the claimant is entitled*".

The Claimant can make early Part 36 offers in Fixed Recoverable Costs cases and the consequences for the Defendant in the Claimant obtaining a more advantageous Judgment at Trial are it can be argued, quite severe for the Defendant:-

36.14

(1) Subject to rule 36.14A, this rule applies where upon judgment being entered –

(a) a claimant fails to obtain a judgment more advantageous than a defendant's Part 36 offer; or

(b) judgment against the defendant is at least as advantageous to the claimant as the proposals contained in a claimant's Part 36 offer.

(1A) For the purposes of paragraph (1), in relation to any money claim or money element of a claim, 'more advantageous' means better in money terms by any amount, however small, and 'at least as advantageous' shall be construed accordingly.

(2) Subject to paragraphs (6) and (7), where rule 36.14(1)(a) applies, the court will, unless it considers it unjust to do so, order that the defendant is entitled to –

(a) costs from the date on which the relevant period expired; and

(b) interest on those costs.

(3) Subject to paragraph (6), where rule 36.14(1)(b) applies, the court will, unless it considers it unjust to do so, order that the claimant is entitled to –

(a) interest on the whole or part of any sum of money (excluding interest) awarded at a rate not exceeding 10% above base rate(GL) for

some or all of the period starting with the date on which the relevant period expired;

(b) his costs on the indemnity basis from the date on which the relevant period expired; and

(c) interest on those costs at a rate not exceeding 10% above base rate[GL]*; and*

(d) an additional amount, which shall not exceed £75,000, calculated by applying the prescribed percentage set out below to an amount which is –

(i) where the claim is or includes a money claim, the sum awarded to the claimant by the court; or

(ii) where the claim is only a non-monetary claim, the sum awarded to the claimant by the court in respect of costs –

Amount awarded by the court	Prescribed percentage
up to £500,000	10% of the amount awarded;
above £500,000 up to £1,000,000	10% of the first £500,000 and 5% of any amount above that figure

It is argued that it is therefore prudent for Claimant lawyers to make early Part 36 offers to encourage Defendants to settle early. This will likely be the only way, it is argued, that Defendants will be encouraged to settle cases within fixed recoverable costs.

Early and realistic Part 36 offers will hold a tactical advantage for the Claimant.

Conclusions

It may be argued that if the majority of Portal Claims continue to exit the low value portal, and are litigated, these types of Claims are likely to remain profitable for Claimant Solicitors. As will be seen from later chapters, Employers' liability cases can be extremely complicated and the danger of using inexperienced Fee Earners can lead to matters being missed, or claims with little or no prospects of success being progressed to litigation. The key to post-Jackson cases is arguably to identify the cases likely to fail very early on. That is what the remainder of this book will concentrate on.

CHAPTER TWO
BASIC PRINCIPLES, NEGLIGENCE, VICARIOUS LIABILITY, CONTROL OF THE WORKPLACE, WHO IS AN EMPLOYEE, THE POSITION AS TO AGENCY WORKERS/SELF-EMPLOYED AND CONTRIBUTORY NEGLIGENCE

Who is an Employee?

Under ERA 1996, an "employee" is defined as an *"individual who has entered into or works under...a contract of employment"*, and a *"contract of employment"* is defined, in turn, to mean *"a contract of service or apprenticeship, whether express or implied, and (if it is express) whether oral or in writing"*. The 1996 Act sets out in full:-

Statement of initial employment particulars.
(1) Where an employee begins employment with an employer, the employer shall give to the employee a written statement of particulars of employment.
(2) The statement may (subject to section 2(4)) be given in instalments and (whether or not given in instalments) shall be given not later than two months after the beginning of the employment.
(3) The statement shall contain particulars of—
(a) the names of the employer and employee,
(b) the date when the employment began, and
(c) the date on which the employee's period of continuous employment began (taking into account any employment with a previous employer which counts towards that period).
(4) The statement shall also contain particulars, as at a specified date not more than seven days before the statement (or the instalment containing them) is given, of—
(a) the scale or rate of remuneration or the method of calculating remuneration,

(b) the intervals at which remuneration is paid (that is, weekly, monthly or other specified intervals),

(c) any terms and conditions relating to hours of work (including any terms and conditions relating to normal working hours),

(d) any terms and conditions relating to any of the following—

(i) entitlement to holidays, including public holidays, and holiday pay (the particulars given being sufficient to enable the employee's entitlement, including any entitlement to accrued holiday pay on the termination of employment, to be precisely calculated),

(ii) incapacity for work due to sickness or injury, including any provision for sick pay, and

(iii) pensions and pension schemes,

(e) the length of notice which the employee is obliged to give and entitled to receive to terminate his contract of employment,

(f) the title of the job which the employee is employed to do or a brief description of the work for which he is employed,

(g) where the employment is not intended to be permanent, the period for which it is expected to continue or, if it is for a fixed term, the date when it is to end,

(h) either the place of work or, where the employee is required or permitted to work at various places, an indication of that and of the address of the employer,

(j) any collective agreements which directly affect the terms and conditions of the employment including, where the employer is not a party, the persons by whom they were made, and

(k) where the employee is required to work outside the United Kingdom for a period of more than one month—

(i) the period for which he is to work outside the United Kingdom,

(ii) the currency in which remuneration is to be paid while he is working outside the United Kingdom,

(iii) any additional remuneration payable to him, and any benefits to be provided to or in respect of him, by reason of his being required to work outside the United Kingdom, and

(iv) any terms and conditions relating to his return to the United Kingdom.

Parties to a contract will often, but not always, put the terms and conditions that govern the relationship into writing. There is no requirement for a contract of employment to be in writing, it can be written, oral or a mixture of both. See *Dacas v Brook Street Bureau (UK) Limited [2004] IRLR*.

In *Lane v Shire Roofing Co (Oxford) Ltd* [1995] *IRLR 493 : [1995] PIQR P417: Times, February 22, 1995* the Claimant was a building worker who was hired by the Defendant Employer to carry out a re-roofing job for which he was to be paid according to a daily rate. The Defendant *"considered it prudent and advantageous to hire for individual jobs"*. While carrying out the work, the Claimant fell and was injured. It was held that he was an Employee for the purposes of the job, and so was owed the common law duty of care with regard to his health and safety. The Court found that the fact that he used his own tools or controlled his work were decisive but the question as to whose business he was engaged in had to be considered. The answer to that question depended on where the financial risk lay and whether and how far the workman had an opportunity of profiting from sound management in the performance of his task. Since the business which the Plaintiff was engaged on was the Defendants' business and not his own, the Defendants owed the duties of employers to the plaintiff. The case is important as it looked a number of key cases which govern the employment relationship and the key passages from the Judgment are as follows in this context:-

> *"The next question is whether the respondents owed to the plaintiff the common law or statutory duty of an employer to his employees, or whether the appellant when doing that job was acting as an independent contractor. When it comes to the question of safety at work, there is a real public interest in recognising the employer/employee relationship when it exists, because of the responsibilities that the common law and statutes such as the Employers' Liability (Compulsory Insurance) Act 1969 places on the employer?*
>
> *The judge was to find that the appellant was not an employee, but was an independent contractor. In that event the appellant would have*

been responsible for his own safety; the respondent would have owed him no duty of care, and would have had no responsibility (statutory or at common law) for the safety of the work done by the appellant.

*We were taken through the standard authorities on this matter: **Readymix Concrete (South East) Ltd. v. Minister of Pensions and National Insurance [1968] 2 QB 497; Market Investigations Ltd. v. Minister of Social Security [1969] 2 QB 173; and Ferguson v. Dawson [1976] 1 WLR 1213**, to name the principal ones. Two general remarks should be made. The overall employment background is very different today (and was, though less so, in 1986) than it had been at the time when those cases were decided. First, for a variety of reasons, there are more self-employed and fewer in employment. There is a greater flexibility in employment, with more temporary and shared employment. Second, there are perceived advantages for both workman and employer in the relationship between them being that of independent contractor. From the workman's point of view, being self-employed brings him into a more benevolent and less prompt taxation regime. From the employer's point of view, the protection of employee's rights contained in the employment protection legislation of the 1970s brought certain perceived disincentives to the employer to take on full-time long term employees. So even in 1986 there were reasons on both sides to avoid the employee label. But, as I have already said, there were, and are, good policy reasons in the safety at work field to ensure that the law properly categorises between employees and independent contractors.*

That line of authority shows that there are many factors to be taken into account in answering this question, and, with different priority being given to those factors in different cases, all depends on the facts of each individual case.

Certain principles relevant to this case, however, emerge.

First, the element of control will be important: who lays down what is to be done, the way in which it is to be done, the means by which it is to be done, and the time when it is done?

Who provides (i.e. hires and fires) the team by which it is done, and who provides the material, plant and machinery and tools used?

*But it is recognised that the control test may not be decisive - for instance, in the case of skilled employees, with discretion to decide how their work should be done. In such cases the question is broadened to whose business was it: was the workman carrying on his own business, or was he carrying on that of his employers? **The American Supreme Court, in United States of America v. Silk (1946) 331 US 704**, asks the question whether the men were employees "as a matter of economic reality". The answer to this question may cover much of the same ground as the control test (such as whether he provides his own equipment and hires his own helpers) **but may involve looking to see where the financial risk lies, and whether and how far he has an opportunity of profiting from sound management in the performance of his task** (see Market Investigations v. Minister of Social Security (supra at page 185).*

And these questions must be asked in the context of who is responsible for the overall safety of the men doing the work in question. Mr. Whittaker, of the respondents, was cross- examined on these lines, and he agreed that he was so responsible. Such an answer is not decisive (though it may be indicative) because ultimately the question is one of law, and he could be wrong as to where the legal responsibility lies".

Thus, in turn, the following questions are likely to establish whether it was an Employer/Employee relationship:-

(1) Was there a written agreement or terms of employment?
(2) If not, was there an oral agreement intended to create an employment relationship?
(3) Did the Employer have control of the premises where the accident took place?
(4) Where does the financial risk lie, in other words, who profits from the task?

(5) Who is responsible for the overall safety of the persons doing the work?

(6) Who provides the materials, plant and machinery, and tools used?

The Control Test – Further Authorities:-

Who had control of where the accident took place? The case of *Performing Rights Society v Mitchell & Booker Ltd (1924)* is of some assistance. The Defendants were sued for the breach of copyright by a jazz band. The Defendant owned a dance-hall and had agreed in writing for a band to play at the hall as long as it did not infringe any copyright in the music it chose to perform. Unfortunately the band chose to play some music but did not have the Plaintiff's permission. The Plaintiff decided to sue the owners of the dance hall looking to hold them responsible for the actions of the band. However the Defendant's liability depended on it being proved that the band were not employed by them. The court looked at the facts that regular hours were worked each day by the band, there was a fixed period of employment, the band had been told where they should work, and they had exclusivity of service. There was also a right to dismiss the band for the breach of any fair instructions or requirement. In short the court looked at the 'nature and degree of detailed control over the person alleged to be a servant' and the band were held to be an employee. The Court held that band members engaged to perform and were employees of the occupier of the dance hall as the agreement "*the right of continuous, dominant, and detailed control on every point, including the nature of the music to be played.*"

In *Gould v Minister of National Insurance (1951) 1 KB 731* at 734, stated "*The real question is one of the degrees of control exercised by the person employing...and this means not only the amount of control but the nature of that control and the direction in which it is exercised*"

In *Stevenson Jordan & Harrison Ltd v Macdonald and Evan [1952] 1 TLR 101* Denning LJ stated, "*...under a contract of service, a man is employed as part of the business, and his work is done as an integral part of* *the business; whereas under a contract for services his work, although done for the business is not integrated into it, but is only accessory to it…".*

The Common Law Duty of Care: A More Detailed Analysis

The common law duty is to take reasonable care to avoid injuring one's neighbours, *Donoghue v Stevenson [1932] AC 562.* Thus, an employer has a reasonable duty to take care for his employees' health and safety. It is contended that this calls for a reasonable response, taking into account the relationship of the parties, the magnitude of the risk of injury that was reasonably foreseeable, the seriousness of the consequences for the person for whom the risk is owed of the risk eventuating and the costs and practicality of preventing the risk (as in *Walker* below). The duty in *Donoghue v Stevenson* is primary and cannot be transferred to someone else, diluted, or delegated to employees.

Wilson & Clyde Co. Limited –v- English 1937 3 ALL ER 628, Lord Wright said that the employer's duty is *"personal to the employer to take reasonable care for the safety of his workmen, whether the employer be an individual, a firm or a company and whether or not the employer takes any share in the conduct of operations".*

Boyle v Kodak Limited [1969 1 WLR 661]. This case is authority for the principle that, where a breach of statutory duty on the part of an employer has been proved, the Claimant is entitled to some damages, even where he is also negligent, unless it can be shown that the employer's breach did not in fact contribute to the accident. Lord Reid cited the following passage from *Ginty v Belmont Building Supplies Ltd [at 666F]:*

> *'In my view, the important and fundamental question in a case like this is not whether there was a delegation, but simply the usual question: whose fault was it? If the answer to that question is that in substance and reality the accident was solely due to the fault of the plaintiff, so that he was the sole author of his own wrong, he is disentitled to recover. But that has to be applied to the particular case*

*and it is not necessarily conclusive for the employer to show that it was a wrongful act of the employee plaintiff which caused the accident. It might also appear from the evidence that something was done or omitted by the employer which caused or contributed to the accident: there may have been lack of proper supervision or lack of proper instructions; the employer may have employed for this purpose some insufficiently experienced men, or he may in the past have acquiesced in some wrong behaviour on the part of the men. Therefore, if one finds that the immediate and direct cause of the accident was some wrongful act of the man, that is not decisive. **One has to enquire whether the fault of the employer under the statutory regulations consists of, and is co-extensive with, the wrongful act of the employee. If there is some fault on the part of the employer which goes beyond or is independent of the wrongful act of the employee, and was the cause of the accident, the employer has some liability.'***

Safe Premises, Plant and Equipment

In *Latimer v AEC Limited [1953] AC643* the Plaintiff was employed by the Defendant. On the afternoon of the day of the accident, an exceptionally heavy rainstorm had flooded the whole of the Defendant's premises. Oil, which normally ran in covered channels in the floor of the building, rose to the surface and when the water drained away, left an oily film on the floor. The Defendants took measures to clean away the oil, using all the sawdust available to them. The Plaintiff came on duty with the night shift, unaware of the condition of the floor. While endeavoring to place a heavy barrel on a trolley, his foot slipped on the still oily surface, he fell on his back, and the barrel crushed his left ankle. The trial judge found a breach of common law duty. The Court of Appeal reversed this decision. The Judgment in Latimer set out:-

Lord Denning observed: "...in every case of foreseeable risk it is a matter of balancing the risk against the measures necessary to eliminate it."

If in *Latimer,* no steps had been taken, the outcome would have been entirely different. An employer therefore has a duty at common law to provide safe premises, plant and equipment.

Safe System of Work

A good example can be found in *Walker v Northumberland County Council [1995] IRLR 35.* The facts are outlined from the Judgment as follows:-

> *"The plaintiff worked for the defendants ("the Council") as an area social services officer from 1970 until December 1987. His position was one in middle management. He was responsible as manager for four teams of social services field workers in the Blyth Valley area of Northumberland. His office was at Cramlington. He in turn was answerable to the Assistant Director of the Field Services Division of the Council's Social Services Department. That was Mr D N Davison. His office was at County Hall, Morpeth. Blyth Valley was one of five social service divisions in Northumberland. It was a predominantly urban area and comprised a new town development at Cramlington with a relatively high proportion of young families with children many of whom had recently acquired houses which had previously been local authority housing. It was an area which because of the social profile of the population was particularly productive of child-care problems falling within the ambit of responsibility of the Social Services Department. Amongst these problems in the course of the 1980s child abuse references were particularly prevalent. The population in Blyth Valley rose during this period and so did the volume of work which had to be undertaken by Mr Walker and his teams of field workers. Although the number of field workers in the area had been increased during the period 1974 to 1978, there was no increase after 1978. By 1986 the pressure of work on those Social Service workers who were working in Blyth Valley had become very considerable. Not only were the teams of field workers under increased pressure, but so was Mr Walker. The stress and anxiety created by that work pressure was intense. The increasing incidence of child abuse cases was particularly stressful for all concerned: for the field workers whose cases they were*

and who had to deal directly with the families and children and for Mr Walker whose responsibility it was to make provision for the adequate manning of such cases by his teams of field social workers and for the holding of case conferences and the production of reports in respect of each child referred to the Department in his area of Blyth Valley.At the end of November 1986 Mr Walker suffered a nervous breakdown. He suffered from mental exhaustion, acute anxiety, head-aches, sleeplessness, irritability, inability to cope with any form of stress and a tendency to weep and to become upset. Under medical advice he remained off work until 4 March 1987. Mr Walker was 50 on 10 March 1987.While off work Mr Walker was treated by his family doctor and was seen by Dr D A Stephens, a very experienced psychi-atrist who had known him professionally for many years by reason of Mr Walker's social services work. Mr Walker had no previous history of mental disorder and Dr Stephens observed that "his anxieties are sharply focused on work pressures, while a comprehensive review of all other areas of his life fail to produce any evidence of concurrent problems". He had known Mr Walker "as a stable, industrious and committed colleague for many years and was surprised to hear about his recent difficulties".

The case is a good example of how the employer was liable at common law, for failing to provide a safe system of work. The key sections from the Judgment are:-

"The plaintiff's case is that the immediate superiors of Mr Walker knew that social work is particularly stressful, that such stress can give rise to mental illness, that the workload falling upon Mr Walker as area officer of the Blyth Valley area was by 1984 such as to impose increasing stress on Mr Walker, that such workload became more stressful during the period 1984-1986 and that accordingly they ought reasonably to have foreseen that, unless they took steps to alleviate the impact of that workload, there was a real risk that Mr Walker would suffer mental illness. In those circum-stances, the Council's duty as employer of Mr Walker being to take reasonable steps to provide a safe system of work, it was in breach of that duty in as much as the system of work was a threat to mental

health which remained un-remedied and caused Mr Walker's mental breakdown.

The Council's case is that, while it concedes that it owed to Mr Walker a general duty to exercise reasonable care to provide him with a reasonably safe working system and to take reasonable steps to protect him from risks which are reasonably foreseeable, there was no breach of that duty: it was not reasonably foreseeable at any material time that Mr Walker's work would impose upon him such stress as to give to a real risk of mental illness and alternatively, if such risk was reasonably foreseeable, the Council did not in all the circumstances, in particular, the budgetary constraints to which the Social Services Department was subject at the time, act unreasonably in failing to relieve the pressure on Mr Walker. Mr Simon Hawkesworth QC, on behalf of the Council has submitted that, in as much as the only effective remedial measures would have involved taking on more staff and therefore the allocation of additional funds for that purpose by the Social Services Department or, indeed the Council itself, and since the application of the Council's limited resources involved policymaking decisions as distinct from operational decisions, the Council cannot be said to have been in breach of any duty of care in having failed to take those decisions.

The Court looked at a number of helpful authorities with regards to foreseeability.

"It is reasonably clear from the authorities that once a duty of care has been established the standard of care required for the performance of that duty must be measured against the yardstick of reasonable conduct on the part of a person in the position of that person who owes the duty. The law does not impose upon him the duty of an insurer against all injury or damage caused by him, however unlikely or unexpected and whatever the practical difficulties of guarding against it. It calls for no more than a reasonable response, what is reasonable being measured by the nature of the neighbourhood relationship, the magnitude of the risk of injury which was reasonably foreseeable, the seriousness of the consequence

for the person to whom the duty is owed of the risk eventuating and the cost and practicability of preventing the risk.

That these are the individual constituents of the yardstick of reasonable conduct is firmly supported by the observations of Lord Thankerton in Glasgow Corporation v Muir [1943] AC 448 at page 454:"In my opinion, it has long been held in Scotland that all that a person can be bound to foresee are the reasonable and probable consequences of the failure to take care, judged by the standard of the ordinary reasonable man....... The court must be careful to place itself in the position of the person charged with the duty and to consider what he or she should have reasonably anticipated as a natural and probable consequence of neglect, and not to give undue weight to the fact that a distressing accident has happened....."To the same effect is the speech of Lord Porter in Bolton v Stone, supra, at page 858:"It is not enough that the event should be such as can reasonably be foreseen. The further result that injury is likely to follow must also be such as a reasonable man would contemplate before he can be convicted of actionable negligence. Nor is the remote possibility of injury occurring enough. There must be sufficient probability to lead a reasonable man to anticipate it. The existence of some risk is an ordinary incident of life, even when all due care has been, as it must be, taken."And in Paris v Stepney Borough Council [1951] AC 367 at page 375 Lord Simonds expressly recognised the potential seriousness of injury as a relevant factor in assessing the standard of care to be expected of the reasonable employer. In Latimer v AEC Ltd [1952] 2 QB 701, Lord Denning observed:"...in every case of foreseeable risk it is a matter of balancing the risk against the measures necessary to eliminate it."and in Overseas Tankship (UK) Ltd v The Miller Steamship Co Ltd [1967] AC 617 at page 542, Lord Reid said:"It does not follow that, no matter what the circumstances may be, it is justifiable to neglect a risk of such a small magnitude. A reasonable man would only neglect such a risk if he had some valid reason for doing so, eg that it would involve considerable expense to eliminate the risk. He would weigh the risk against the difficulty of eliminating it."The practicability of remedial measures must clearly take into account the resources and facilities at the disposal of the person or body owing the duty of care: see Lord Reid in British Railways Board v Herrington [1972] AC 877 *at page 899, and the purpose of the activity which has given rise to the risk of injury: the risk must be balanced "against the end to be achieved": see Denning LJ in* Watt v Hertfordshire CC [1954] 1 WLR 835 *at page 838. of harm".*

In Walker the Court concluded, finding the Defendant liable:-

"That said, the duty of an employer public body, whether in contract or tort, to provide a safe system of work is, as I have said, a duty only to do what is reasonable, and in many cases it may be necessary to take into account decisions which are within the policy-making area and the reasons for those decisions in order to test whether the body's conduct has been reasonable. In that exercise there can be no basis for treating the public body differently in principle *from any other commercial employer, although there would have to be taken into account considerations such as budgetary constraints and perhaps lack of flexibility of decision-taking which might not arise with a commercial employer.Having regard to the reasonably foreseeable size of the risk of repetition of Mr Walker's illness if his duties were not alleviated by effective additional assistance and to the reasonably foreseeable gravity of the mental breakdown which might result if nothing were done, I have come to the conclusion that the standard of care to be expected of a reasonable local authority required that in March 1987 such additional assistance should be provided if not on a permanent basis, at least until restructuring of the Social Services had been effected and the workload on Mr Walker thereby permanently reduced. That measure of additional assistance ought to have been provided notwithstanding that it could be expected to have some disruptive effect on the Council's provision of services to the public. When Mr Walker returned from his first illness the Council had to decide whether it was prepared to go on employing him in spite of the fact that he had made it sufficiently clear that he must have effective additional help if he was to continue at Blyth Valley. It chose to continue to employ him, but provided no effective help. In so doing it was, in my judgment, acting unreasonably and therefore in breach of its duty of care.I understand it to be accepted that if there was breach of*

duty damage was caused by that breach. However, in view of the fact that I have decided this case on the second breakdown alone, it is right to add that I am satisfied on the evidence that had the further assistance been provided to Mr Walker, his second breakdown would probably not have occurred. In the event, there will be judgment for the plaintiff on liability with damages yet to be assessed".

Health and Safety at Work Etc Act 1974 Further Information

Breach of the Regulations under the 1974 Act does not in itself afford a cause of action. The Act sets out:-

2 General duties of employers to their employees.
(1) It shall be the duty of every employer to ensure, so far as is reasonably practicable, the health, safety and welfare at work of all his employees.
(2) Without prejudice to the generality of an employer's duty under the preceding subsection, the matters to which that duty extends include in particular—
(a) the provision and maintenance of plant and systems of work that are, so far as is reasonably practicable, safe and without risks to health;
(b) arrangements for ensuring, so far as is reasonably practicable, safety and absence of risks to health in connection with the use, handling, storage and transport of articles and substances;
(c) the provision of such information, instruction, training and supervision as is necessary to ensure, , the health and safety at work of his employees;
(d) so far as is reasonably practicable as regards any place of work under the employer's control, the maintenance of it in a condition that is safe and without risks to health and the provision and maintenance of means of access to and egress from it that are safe and without such risks;
(e) the provision and maintenance of a working environment for his employees that is, so far as is reasonably practicable, safe, without risks to health, and adequate as regards facilities and arrangements for their welfare at work.

(3) Except in such cases as may be prescribed, it shall be the duty of every employer to prepare and as often as may be appropriate revise a written statement of his general policy with respect to the health and safety at work of his employees and the organisation and arrangements for the time being in force for carrying out that policy, and to bring the statement and any revision of it to the notice of all of his employees.

The burden of proving that compliance with an obligation was not 'reasonably practical' is on the Defendant as per section 40 which sets out:-

40 Onus of proving limits of what is practicable etc.
In any proceedings for an offence under any of the relevant statutory provisions consisting of a failure to comply with a duty or requirement to do something so far as is practicable or so far as is reasonably practicable, or to use the best practicable means to do something, it shall be for the accused to prove (as the case may be) that it was not practicable or not reasonably practicable to do more than was in fact done to satisfy the duty or requirement, or that there was no better practicable means than was in fact used to satisfy the duty or requirement.

By section 15 of the Regulations, the Secretary of State has the power to make Health and Safety Regulations. Breach of the Regulations, gives rise to civil liability (for accidents before October 2013 as set out in the ERRA chapter), unless the Regulations states otherwise (see section 74).

Self-Employed Individuals and Agency Workers

Difficulties can sometimes arise in the context of self-employed workers and agency workers, as to who had the duty of care in such circumstances.

In the case of agency workers, sometimes a worker will be employed by an agency and be sent to work at the site of the client. In these circumstances the case of *ROBERT PAUL BAILEY V (1) COMMAND SECURITY SERVICES LTD (2) TJX INC (USA) (A FIRM) (2001)* where Liability was established and apportioned between the employer of the claimant and the owner of the warehouse in which he was injured when he fell down an unguarded lift shaft assists. In this case, the first defendant, the employer, had failed to carry out a risk assessment of the warehouse, where a security guard had sustained injury, where it had never visited the premises of the client. Thus, *Bailey* indicates that an agency may be liable to some extent, if its risk assessment was inadequate, and it had not carried out a site survey, before sending the Claimant to work there, which in this case may have revealed the lack of safety equipment in my view. The Court said that the first Defendant owed no duty under Reg.13 of the Regulations because the accident site was not under its control at the relevant time. However, the first Defendant was negligent in that it did not carry out any thorough risk assessment of the premises. If it had, it would have recognised that the unguarded lift shaft posed a danger to its employees.

A similar problem sometimes arises in the context of self employed contractors working on, for example, building sites. Whilst sub-contractors are responsible for their own safety, if the main occupier/contractor is negligent in providing a safe workplace or site location, the main contractor may be liable for an Accident at Work claim. In this context the control test becomes important, and whether the contractor was working on a site controlled by a third party and/or under the direction of a third party. The reader is referred to the control section of this chapter in this context. Section 3 of the Health and Safety at Work Act 1974 sets out as follows:-

> ### General duties of employers and self-employed to persons other than their employees.
> *(1) It shall be the duty of every employer to conduct his undertaking in such a way as to ensure, so far as is reasonably practicable, that persons not in his employment who may be affected thereby are not thereby exposed to risks to their health or safety.*
> *(2) It shall be the duty of every self-employed person to conduct his undertaking in such a way as to ensure, so far as is reasonably practicable, that he and other persons (not being his employees) who may be affected thereby are not thereby exposed to risks to their health or safety.*

(3) In such cases as may be prescribed, it shall be the duty of every employer and every self-employed person, in the prescribed circumstances and in the prescribed manner, to give to persons (not being his employees) who may be affected by the way in which he conducts his undertaking the prescribed information about such aspects of the way in which he conducts his undertaking as might affect their health or safety.

In *R v Associated Octel Co Limited [1997]*, the court looked at the liability of independent contractors and found the employer was liable. RGP Ltd was convicted of an offence under section 2 of the 1974 Act, and Octel Ltd of an offence under section 3. Octel Ltd appealed to the Court of Appeal. It was argued on their behalf that section 3 did not involve liability for the actions of independent contractors.

The court ruled that it was a question of fact in each case whether an activity which caused a risk to the health and safety of persons (other than employees) amounted to the conduct of an undertaking. The term "undertaking" was taken as meaning "enterprise" or "business" and the cleaning, maintenance or repair of plant, machinery or buildings necessary for carrying on the business was part of the undertaking (whether carried out by the client's employees or by an independent contractor). Therefore Octel Ltd was liable under section 3(1).

Contributory Negligence

Section 7 of the Health and Safety at Work etc 1974 sets out:-

7 General duties of employees at work.
It shall be the duty of every employee while at work—
(a) to take reasonable care for the health and safety of himself and of other persons who may be affected by his acts or omissions at work; and
(b) as regards any duty or requirement imposed on his employer or any other person by or under any of the relevant statutory provisions, to co-operate with him so far as is necessary to enable that duty or requirement to be performed or complied with.

In *Jones –v- Lovox Quarries Limited 1952 2QB 608* Denning LJ said *"a person is guilty of contributory negligence if you ought reasonably to have foreseen that if he did not act as a reasonable, prudent man, he might hurt himself, and in his reckonings he must take into account the possibility of others being careless. If a man carelessly rides on a vehicle in a dangerous position and subsequently there is a collision in which his injuries are made worse by reason of his position than they would otherwise have been, then his damage is partly the result of his own fault and the damages recoverable by him to be reduced accordingly. In my opinion, even if the Court was to find primary liability on behalf of the First Defendant, in respect of the issues regarding lack of training records and risk assessments, in my opinion there is a potential for up to 50% contributory negligence on behalf of the Claimant for the reasons set out above".*

Anderson v Newham College of Further Education [2003] ICR 212. In that case the Judge found that the Defendant employers were in breach of statutory duty under regulation 12(3) of the Workplace (Health, Safety and Welfare) Regulations 1992 because a whiteboard in a classroom was stored in a dangerous position so as to create a tripping hazard. The judge also held that the Claimant employee was contributorily negligent in failing to see and avoid the hazard and reduced his damages by 90%. The Court of Appeal held that:-

> *'Whether a claim was in negligence or breach of statutory duty, if the evidence showed the entire fault to lie with the claimant, there was no liability on the defendant and section 1(1) of the Law Reform (Contributory Negligence) Act 1945 did not bite: if there was liability, contributory negligence could reduce its monetary quantification under section 1(1) but could not legally or logically nullify it; but that a high standard of proof was required to shift the entire blame for a breach of statutory duty from an employer to an injured employee...and that the fair apportionment of liability by reason of contributory negligence was 50%'*

Thus, it is always necessary to consider the issue of contributory negligence in any claim. For example,

1. Did the Claimant know the act he was undertaking was dangerous?
2. If the Claimant was trained or was in a Senior position, should he have known the act he was undertaking was dangerous?

Conclusions

As can be seen, the law in this area is extremely complex, and this chapter is designed to provide the reader with the basics, and a range of cases that can assist as a starting point to an investigation. The remaining chapters will discuss the Regulations and investigating various types of accidents at work in more detail, including establishing liability.

CHAPTER THREE
EARLY INVESTIGATIONS INTO LIABILITY: PRE-ACTION PROTOCOLS AND EARLY DISCLOSURE, GATHERING EVIDENCE TO PROVE THE CASE AND PART 36/LITIGATION TACTICS

It is clear that in relation to post-Jackson, post 31 July 2013 Employers' Liability cases, the incentives for Defendants and Insurers to settle these cases have now been substantially reduced. These cases are now subject to portal and fixed recoverable costs and as we have seen from the previous chapter, the insurer can now run three or four of these claims to trial and lose them, for effectively the same costs as running one CFA claim to trial, with a 100% uplift under the pre-Jackson regime and losing that at trial.

This new litigation landscape of course poses enormous difficulties for Claimant lawyers. The '50/50' cases that previously that may have been issued and settled, before trial, arguably are no longer likely to happen. This means that law firms more than ever, will have to be careful to vet claims more carefully before taking them on. To run a profitable department post-Jackson, the majority of claims will have to succeed, given there is no longer the flexibility of CFA uplifts to cushion the shortfalls of the cases that are lost at trial.

This chapter deals with using the new amendments to the CPR post April 2013 and post July 2013, when the Jackson reforms came into effect to a) vet cases early on, b) obtain disclosure quickly and, c) settling the case before it gets to trial and how Part 36 can encourage that.

Pre-Action Protocols

If a case exits the Low Value Portal i.e. because liability has been denied or liability has not been admitted by the defendant (or for any other reason), then the case will still fall within the Personal Injury Pre-Action Protocol which says:-

> *"3.7 The **defendant**('s insurers) will have a **maximum of three months** from the date of acknowledgment of the claim **to investigate**. No later than the end of that period the defendant (insurer) shall reply, stating whether liability is denied and, if so, giving reasons for their denial of liability including any alternative version of events relied upon"*

Further it goes on:-

> *"3.10 If the **defendant denies liability**, he should enclose with the letter of reply, **documents** in his possession which are **material to the issues** between the parties, and which would be likely to be ordered to be disclosed by the court, either on an application for pre-action disclosure, or on disclosure during proceedings.*
>
> *3.11 Attached at Annex B are **specimen**, but non-exhaustive, **lists** of documents likely to be material in different types of claims. Where the claimant's investigation of the case is well advanced, the letter of claim could indicate which classes of documents are considered relevant for early disclosure. Alternatively these could be identified at a later stage.*
>
> *3.12 Where the defendant admits primary liability, but alleges contributory negligence by the claimant, the defendant should give reasons supporting those allegations and disclose those documents from Annex B which are relevant to the issues in dispute. The claimant should respond to the allegations of contributory negligence before proceedings are issued".*

Pre-Action Protocols Disclosure

The Pre-Action Protocol for Employers' Liability Claims suggests the following disclosure should be provided by the Defendant, once the claim has fallen out of the Portal. The type of disclosure will depend upon the facts:-

WORKPLACE CLAIMS
GENERAL DOCUMENTS

(i) accident book entry;

(ii) other entries in the book or other accident books, relating to accidents or injuries similar to those suffered by our client (and if it is contended there are no such entries please confirm we may have facilities to inspect all accident books);

(iii) first aider report;

(iv) surgery record;

(v) foreman/supervisor accident report;

(vi) safety representative's accident report;

(vii) RIDDOR (Reporting of Injuries, Diseases and Dangerous Occurrences Regulations) reported to HSE or relevant investigatory agency;

(viii) back to work interview notes and report;

(ix) all personnel/occupational health records relating to our client;

(x) other communications between defendants and HSE or other relevant

investigatory agency;

(xi) minutes of Health and Safety Committee meeting(s) where accident/matter

considered;

(xii) copies of all relevant CCTV footage and any other relevant photographs, videos and/or DVDs;

(xiii) copies of all electronic communications/documentation relating to the accident;

(xiv) earnings information where defendant is employer;

(xv) reports to DWP;

(xvi) manufacturer's or dealers instructions or recommendations concerning use of

the work equipment;

(xvii) service or maintenance records of the work equipment;

(xviii) all documents recording arrangements for detecting, removing or cleaning up any articles or substances on the floor of the premises likely to cause a trip or slip;

(xix) work sheets and all other documents completed by or on behalf of those *responsible for implementing the cleaning policy and recording work done;*

(xx) all invoices, receipts and other documents relating to the purchase of relevant

safety equipment to prevent a repetition of the accident;

(xxi) all correspondence, memoranda or other documentation received or brought

into being concerning the condition or repair of the work equipment/the premises;

(xxii) all correspondence, instructions, estimates, invoices and other documentation submitted or received concerning repairs, remedial works or other works to the work equipment/the premises since the date of that accident;

(xxiii) work sheets and all other documents recording work done completed by those responsible for maintaining the work equipment/premises;

(xxiv) all relevant risk assessments;

(xxv) all reports, conclusions or recommendations following any enquiry or investigation into the accident;

(xxvi) the record kept of complaints made by employees together with all other documents recording in any way such complaints or actions taken thereon;

(xxvii) all other correspondence sent, or received, relating to our client's injury prior to receipt of this letter of claim;

(xxviii) documents listed above relating to any previous/similar accident/matter

identified by the claimant and relied upon as proof of negligence including accident

book entries;

WORKPLACE CLAIMS – DISCLOSURE WHERE SPECIFIC REGULATIONS APPLY
SECTION A –

Management of Health and Safety at Work Regulations 1999
Documents including—
(i) Pre-accident Risk Assessment required by Regulation 3(1);

(ii) Post-accident Re-Assessment required by Regulation 3(2);
(iii) Accident Investigation Report prepared in implementing the requirements of
Regulations 4, and 5;
(iv) Health Surveillance Records in appropriate cases required by Regulation 6;
(v) documents relating to the appointment of competent persons to assist required by Regulation 7;
(vi) documents relating to the employees health and safety training required by
Regulation 8;
(vii) documents relating to necessary contacts with external services required by
Regulation 9;
(viii) information provided to employees under Regulation 10.

SECTION B–

Workplace (Health Safety and Welfare) Regulations 1992
Documents including—
(i) repair and maintenance records required by Regulation 5;
(ii) housekeeping records to comply with the requirements of Regulation 9;
(iii) hazard warning signs or notices to comply with Regulation 17 (Traffic Routes).

SECTION C –

Provision and Use of Work Equipment Regulations 1998
Documents including—
(i) manufacturers' specifications and instructions in respect of relevant work
equipment establishing its suitability to comply with Regulation 4;
(ii) maintenance log/maintenance records required to comply with Regulation 5;
(iii) documents providing information and instructions to employees to comply with

Regulation 8;
(iv) documents provided to the employee in respect of training for use to comply with Regulation 9;
(v) risk assessments/documents required to comply with Regulation 12;
(vi) any notice, sign or document relied upon as a defence to alleged breaches of
Regulations 14 to 18 dealing with controls and control systems;
(vii) instruction/training documents issued to comply with the requirements of
Regulation 22 insofar as it deals with maintenance operations where the machinery
is not shut down;
(viii) copies of markings required to comply with Regulation 23;
(ix) copies of warnings required to comply with Regulation 24.

SECTION D –

Personal Protective Equipment at Work Regulations 1992
Documents including—
(i) documents relating to the assessment of the Personal Protective Equipment to
comply with Regulation 6;
(ii) documents relating to the maintenance and replacement of Personal Protective
Equipment to comply with Regulation 7;
(iii) record of maintenance procedures for Personal Protective Equipment to comply
with Regulation 7;
(iv) records of tests and examinations of Personal Protective Equipment to comply
with Regulation 7;
(v) documents providing information, instruction and training in relation to the
Personal Protective Equipment to comply with Regulation 9;
(vi) instructions for use of Personal Protective Equipment to include the manufacturers' instructions to comply with Regulation 10.

SECTION E –

Manual Handling Operations Regulations 1992
Documents including—
(i) Manual Handling Risk Assessment carried out to comply with the requirements of Regulation 4(1)(b)(i);
(ii) re-assessment carried out post-accident to comply with requirements of
Regulation 4(1)(b)(i);
(iii) documents showing the information provided to the employee to give general
indications related to the load and precise indications on the weight of the load and
the heaviest side of the load if the centre of gravity was not positioned centrally to
comply with Regulation 4(1)(b)(iii);
(iv) documents relating to training in respect of manual handling oper-ations and
training records.

SECTION F –

Health and Safety (Display Screen Equipment) Regulations 1992
Documents including—
(i) analysis of work stations to assess and reduce risks carried out to comply with the requirements of Regulation 2;
(ii) re-assessment of analysis of work stations to assess and reduce risks following
development of symptoms by the claimant;
(iii) documents detailing the provision of training including training records to comply with the requirements of Regulation 6;
(iv) documents providing information to employees to comply with the requirements of Regulation 7.

SECTION H –

Construction (Design and Management) Regulations 2007

Documents including—
(i) notification of a project form (HSE F10) to comply with the requirements of
Regulation 7;
(ii) Health and Safety Plan to comply with requirements of Regulation 15;
(iii) Health and Safety file to comply with the requirements of Regulations 12 and 14;
(iv) information and training records provided to comply with the requirements of
Regulation 17;
(v) records of advice from and views of persons at work to comply with the
requirements of Regulation 18;
(vi) reports of inspections made in accordance with Regulation 33;
(vii) records of checks for the purposes of Regulation 34;
(viii) emergency procedures for the purposes of Regulation 39.

SECTION I –

Construction (Health, Safety & Welfare) Regulations 1996
Documents including—
(i) documents produced to comply with requirements of the Regulations.

SECTION J –

Work at Height Regulations 2005
Documents including—
(i) documents relating to planning, supervision and safety carried out for Regulation 4;
(ii) documents relating to training for the purposes of Regulation 5;
(iii) documents relating to the risk assessment carried out for Regulation 6;
(iv) documents relating to the selection of work equipment for the purposes of
Regulation 7;

(v) notices or other means in writing warning of fragile surfaces for the purposes of
Regulation 9;
(vi) documents relating to any inspection carried out for Regulation 12;
(vii) documents relating to any inspection carried out for Regulation 13;
(viii) reports made for the purposes of Regulation 14;
(ix) any certificate issued for the purposes of Regulation 15.

It is advisable that the letter requesting the disclosure is sent as soon as the case exits the portal, then a further request is made 14 days before the end of the protocol period and a final request at the end of the protocol period. Each request should say that if the FULL documents are not disclosed an application will be made for Pre-Action Disclosure at the end of the protocol period, and the costs sought of the application, without any further recourse or warning. This will give the Defendant plenty of notice of the application and should give the Claimant some chance of recovering the costs of the application at the hearing. It should be borne in mind that on a PAD application, the general rule is that the party making the disclosure gets the costs of the application unless there has been some unreasonable conduct in responding to the disclosure requests. This is why these letters are important in terms of the costs of the application.

If the Defendant says it does not hold a document, it should be asked to sign a disclosure statement, with an appropriate statement of truth, to say the document is not available.

The Pre-Action Disclosure Application

Pre-Action Disclosure applications are arguably one of the most common applications in Personal Injury litigation. Unlike a road traffic claim, the Defendant's disclosure is almost always required to assess a potential defence to an Employer's Liability Claim.

The CPR sets out: -

Disclosure before proceedings start

> *"31.16*
> *(1) This rule applies where an application is made to the court under any Act for disclosure before proceedings have started1.*
> *(2) The application must be supported by evidence.*
> *(3) The court may make an order under this rule only where:-*
> *(a) the respondent is likely to be a party to subsequent proceedings;*
> *(b) the applicant is also likely to be a party to those proceedings;*
> *(c) if proceedings have started, the respondent's duty by way of standard disclosure, set out in rule 31.6, would extend to the documents or classes of documents of which the applicant seeks disclosure; and*
> *(d) disclosure before proceedings have started is desirable in order to:-*
> *(i) dispose fairly of the anticipated proceedings;*
> *(ii) assist the dispute to be resolved without proceedings; or*
> *(iii) save costs.*
> *(4) An order under this rule must:-*
> *(a) specify the documents or the classes of documents which the respondent must disclose; and*
> *(b) require him, when making disclosure, to specify any of those documents:-*
> *(i) which are no longer in his control; or*
> *(ii) in respect of which he claims a right or duty to withhold inspection.*
> *(5) Such an order may:-*
> *(a) require the respondent to indicate what has happened to any documents which are no longer in his control; and*
> *(b) specify the time and place for disclosure and inspection".*

It is arguable that as soon as the case reaches the end of the protocol period, if full disclosure has not been provided to enable the Claimant's lawyer to assess the claim, an application should be made immediately given a) the Claimant's lawyer within fixed costs needs the documents to assess the prospects of success, b) a decision cannot be reached without those documents and, c) the Pre-Action Protocols (in most scenarios) are very specific as to what should be disclosed pre-issue.

In making the application it is important that the application sets out in detail a) what the accident circumstances are, b) the nature of the Claimant's investigations, c) what response the Defendant has made to the request and, d) most importantly, why each of the documents are required.

The majority of PAD applications, in the author's experience, settle before they ever get to a hearing, but it is clear post-Jackson that it is more important than ever that disclosure is given in full and on time, so Claimant lawyers can make quick and efficient decisions about which cases are to be closed and the ones that are to be litigated. It must be the case that with Fixed Recoverable Costs, it will no longer be efficient to chase Defendants for documents for months or even years and for cases which are likely to have less than 50% prospects to be sat in Claimant lawyer's cabinets waiting for disclosure to come in order to assess them.

Part 36 – Making the Defendant Settle, Once Out Of The Low Value Portal For Post 31 July 2013 Cases

Post-Jackson, one of the only ways that the Defendant may be encouraged to settle an Employer's Liability case, or any other claim for that matter which stays within fixed costs may be by way of the new Part 36 rules, which came into effect in July 2013, and these are set out as follows:-

> *Costs consequences following judgment- Trial / Disposal*
> *36.14*
> *(1) Subject to rule 36.14A, this rule applies whereupon judgment being entered:-*
> *(b) judgment against the defendant is at least as advantageous to the claimant as the proposals contained in a claimant's Part 36 offer.*
> *(1A) For the purposes of paragraph (1), in relation to any money claim or money element of a claim, 'more advantageous' means better in money terms by any amount, however small, and 'at least as advantageous' shall be construed accordingly.*

> *(3) Subject to paragraph (6), where rule 36.14(1)(b) applies, the court will, unless it considers it unjust to do so, order that the claimant is entitled to –*
> *(a) interest on the whole or part of any sum of money (excluding interest) awarded at a rate not exceeding 10% above base rate for some or all of the period starting with the date on which the relevant period expired;*
> *(b) his costs on the indemnity basis from the date on which the relevant period expired;*
> *(c) interest on those costs at a rate not exceeding 10% above base rate; and*
> *(d) an additional amount, which shall not exceed £75,000, calculated by applying the prescribed percentage set out below to an amount which is –*
> *(ii) where the claim is only a non-monetary claim, the sum awarded to the claimant by the court in respect of costs –*

It is therefore argued that early Part 36 offers on these cases are essential, as this is now the only way Defendants will be encouraged to settle claims, as the costs consequences for the defendant are severe, if the claimant beats its own Part 36 offer at trial. It may be advisable therefore that a realistic Part 36 offer should be made as soon as possible, and as soon as possible after directions have been given and the claim has been allocated to track. As a matter of tactics, the Claimant may however wish to wait until the claim has been allocated before making the offer, since if the case is allocated to the multi track, fixed recoverable costs will not apply.

It is important that the Part 36 offer is a realistic one, rather than as a starting point of negotiations. The earlier the Part 36 offer is made, the greater the consequences for the Defendant, if the offer is not beaten at Trial, and thus the more weight the Defendant is likely to give to that offer when considering whether to accept it or not.

Defendant Part 36 Rules In Post July 2013 FRC Cases

It is still the case that for cases that stay allocated to the fast track and thus within fixed recoverable costs, Defendant Part 36 offers will still apply and thus still 'bite'. It therefore may still be prudent for the claimant to obtain ATE cover to insure the risk.

Costs consequences following judgment
36.14
(1) Subject to rule 36.14A, this rule applies whereupon judgment being entered:-
*(a) **a claimant fails to obtain a judgment more advantageous than a defendant's Part 36 offer;** or*
(1A) For the purposes of paragraph (1), in relation to any money claim or money element of a claim, 'more advantageous' means better in money terms by any amount, however small, and 'at least as advantageous' shall be construed accordingly.
*(2) **Subject to paragraph (6), where rule 36.14(1)(a) applies, the court will, unless it considers it unjust to do so, order that the defendant is entitled to:-***
(a) his costs from the date on which the relevant period expired; and
(b) interest on those costs.

But if the Defendants' costs
45.29F

(1) In this rule:-
(a) paragraphs (8) and (9) apply to assessments of defendants' costs under Part 36;
2) If, in any case to which this Section applies, the court makes an order for costs in favour of the defendant:-
(a) the court will have regard to; and
(b) the amount of costs ordered to be paid shall not exceed,
the amount which would have been payable by the defendant if an order for costs had been made in favour of the claimant at the same stage of the proceedings.

(3) For the purpose of assessing the costs payable to the defendant by reference to the fixed costs in Table 6, Table 6A, Table 6B, Table 6C and Table 6D, "value of the claim for damages" and "damages" shall be treated as references to the value of the claim.

In other words, if the Claimant fails to obtain a judgment more advantageous than a Defendant's Part 36 offer, then unless the court considers it unjust, the Claimant gets the fixed costs under the relevant table up to the stage the case had reached at the end of the relevant period, but must pay the Defendant's costs from the end of the relevant period to the date of judgment, subject to capping.

Where a Defendant is awarded costs, the maximum amount of costs payable by the Claimant to the Defendant is the difference between the fixed costs applicable at the date of acceptance less the costs to which the claimant is entitled.

Allocation Post July 2013 cases

It may be argued therefore, that allocation will become the new battleground between Claimants and Defendants. Claimants will want the case allocated to the multi track, to escape fixed recoverable costs, and Defendants will want the case allocated to the fast track to keep within fixed recoverable costs. The difficulty for claimants is that the Court is now likely to view the majority of Employers' Liability cases as straightforward ones that can be dealt with in the fast track but CPR 26.8 sets out:-

Matters relevant to allocation to a track

26.8
(1) When deciding the track for a claim, the matters to which the court shall have regard include:-
(a) the financial value, if any, of the claim;
(b) the nature of the remedy sought;
(c) the likely complexity of the facts, law or evidence;
(d) the number of parties or likely parties;

(e) the value of any counterclaim or other Part 20 claim and the complexity of any matters relating to it;

(f) the amount of oral evidence which may be required;

(g) the importance of the claim to persons who are not parties to the proceedings;

(h) the views expressed by the parties; and

(i) the circumstances of the parties.

Given that the Court in most cases now allocates initially on paper to a track, it may be a good idea that if a claim is a) complex in law, b) complex in fact, c) requires numerous experts, d) is likely to require oral expert evidence or, e) is going to last more than one day due to the number of witnesses, the Claimant drafts submissions and returns these to the court, with the directions questionnaire and asks for the matter to be listed for a CMC, to determine the issue of track, if the Claimant wants the claim to be allocated to the multi track. The general rule is that if the case is likely to last more than one day, it needs to be allocated to the multi track. It may be advisable that if the case is likely to last more than one day, a draft trial timetable is submitted to the court, setting out why and how.

Many more complex Employers' Liability cases, particularly where there may be multiple Defendants, more serious injuries, or where there are complex disputes of fact, should be in the multi track, to allow provision for expert evidence on both fact and causation, if required. Whatever track a case remains in, and even if it remains within FRC, a Claimant lawyer still of course has a duty to obtain all appropriate evidence to support the case and investigate to the fullest extent, even if it remains within FRCs. It may well be that Defendants are prepared to sacrifice their own medical expert, to keep cases out of the multi track and in FRC. It will be of interest to see how this develops.

Summary

It seems clear that there are a number of tactical decisions to be made early on in Employers Liability cases post-Jackson, and in particular issues surrounding allocation of track, when to make a Part 36 offer and when to make applications for disclosure. However, if one makes astute tactical decisions this will still make this type of work economical for Claimant law firms and to allow claimants continued Access to Justice.

CHAPTER FOUR
THE ENTERPRISE AND REGULATORY REFORM ACT 2013 AND THE IMPACT ON EMPLOYERS' LIABILITY CLAIMS

Section 69 of the Enterprise and Regulatory Reform Act 2013 (ERRA) is now in force. The effect of Section 69 is that most employees seeking compensation for injuries suffered as a result of accidents at work on or after 1 October 2013 will no longer be able solely to rely on a breach of health and safety regulations to establish breach of duty. Instead, they will only be able to seek compensation where it can be shown that the employer has breached the common law duty of care.

Under the 'six pack' Regulations which came into place in 1992, to allow the UK to comply with various European Directives, the employer could find themselves liable, for example, for defective work equipment, even where it had been maintained and inspected properly. The aim of the legislation is to remove the time and cost of the burden of complying with the Regulations from employers. This will arguably make it more difficult for Claimants to succeed in EL claims.

Section 69 of the Act sets out as follows:-

> ***Civil liability for breach of health and safety duties***
> *(1) Section 47 of the Health and Safety at Work etc. Act 1974 (civil liability) is amended as set out in subsections (2) to (7).*
> *(2) In subsection (1), omit paragraph (b) (including the "or" at the end of that paragraph).*
> *(3) For subsection (2) substitute—*
> *"(2) Breach of a duty imposed by a statutory instrument containing (whether alone or with other provision) health and safety regulations shall not be actionable except to the extent that regulations under this section so provide.*
> *(2A) Breach of a duty imposed by an existing statutory provision shall not be actionable except to the extent that regulations under this section*

so provide (including by modifying any of the existing statutory provisions).

(2B) Regulations under this section may include provision for—

(a) a defence to be available in any action for breach of the duty mentioned in subsection (2) or (2A);

(b) any term of an agreement which purports to exclude or restrict any liability for such a breach to be void."

(4) In subsection (3), omit the words from ", whether brought by virtue of subsection (2)" to the end.

(5) In subsection (4)—

(a) for "and (2)" substitute ", (2) and (2A)", and

(b) for "(3)" substitute "(2B)(a)".

(6) Omit subsections (5) and (6).

(7) After subsection (6) insert—

"(7) The power to make regulations under this section shall be exercisable by the Secretary of State."

(8) Where, on the commencement of this section, there is in force an Order in Council made under section 84(3) of the Health and Safety at Work etc. Act 1974 that applies to matters outside Great Britain any of the provisions of that Act that are amended by this section, that Order is to be taken as applying those provisions as so amended.

(9) The amendments made by this section do not apply in relation to breach of a duty which it would be within the legislative competence of the Scottish Parliament to impose by an Act of that Parliament.

(10) The amendments made by this section do not apply in relation to breach of a duty where that breach occurs before the commencement of this section.

The explanatory notes to the ERRA also state: *"The amendment... reverses the present position on civil liability, with the effect, unless any exceptions apply, that it will only be possible to claim for compensation in relation to affected health and safety legislation where it can be proved that the duty holder (usually the employer) has been negligent. This means that in future, for all relevant claims, duty-holders will only have to defend themselves against negligence."*

A Historical Perspective

In order to look at the impact upon Employers' Liability Claims, it is necessary to look at matters from a historical perspective. The new Regulations make changes to section 15 and 47 (2) of the *Health and Safety at Work Act 1974* which sets out:-

> *15 Health and safety regulations.*
> *[F34(1) Subject to the provisions of section 50, the Secretary of State F35. . . shall have power to make regulations under this section for any of the general purposes of this Part (and regulations so made are in this Part referred to as "health and safety regulations").]*
> *(2) Without prejudice to the generality of the preceding subsection, health and safety regulations may for any of the general purposes of this Part make provision for any of the purposes mentioned in Schedule 3.*
> *(3) Health and safety regulations—*
> *(a) may repeal or modify any of the existing statutory provisions;*
> *(b) may exclude or modify in relation to any specified class of case any of the provisions of sections 2 to 9 or any of the existing statutory provisions;*
> *(c) may make a specified authority or class of authorities responsible, to such extent as may be specified, for the enforcement of any of the relevant statutory provisions.*
> *(4) Health and safety regulations—*
> *(a) may impose requirements by reference to the approval of [F36the Executive] or any other specified body or person;*
> *(b) may provide for references in the regulations to any specified document to operate as reference to that document as revised or re-issued from time to time.*
> *(5) Health and safety regulations—*
> *(a) may provide (either unconditionally or subject to conditions, and with or without limit of time) for exemptions from any requirement or prohibition imposed by or under any of the relevant statutory provisions;*
> *(b) may enable exemptions from any requirement or prohibition imposed by or under any of the relevant statutory provisions to be granted (either unconditionally or subject to conditions, and with or*

without limit of time) by any specified person or by any person authorised in that behalf by a specified authority.

(6) Health and safety regulations—

(a) may specify the persons or classes of persons who, in the event of a contravention of a requirement or prohibition imposed by or under the regulations, are to be guilty of an offence, whether in addition to or to the exclusion of other persons or classes of persons;

(b) may provide for any specified defence to be available in proceedings for any offence under the relevant statutory provisions either generally or in specified circumstances;

(c) may exclude proceedings on indictment in relation to offences consisting of a contravention of a requirement or prohibition imposed by or under any of the existing statutory provisions, sections 2 to 9 or health and safety regulations;

(d) may restrict the punishments [F37(other than the maximum fine on conviction on indictment)] which can be imposed in respect of any such offence as is mentioned in paragraph (c) above.

[F38(e)

F39. . . . .]

(7) Without prejudice to section 35, health and safety regulations may make provision for enabling offences under any of the relevant statutory provisions to be treated as having been committed at any specified place for the purpose of bringing any such offence within the field of responsibility of any enforcing authority or conferring jurisdiction on any court to entertain proceedings for any such offence.

(8) Health and safety regulations may take the form of regulations applying to particular circumstances only or to a particular case only (for example, regulations applying to particular premises only).

47 Civil liability.

(1) Nothing in this Part shall be construed—

(a) as conferring a right of action in any civil proceedings in respect of any failure to comply with any duty imposed by sections 2 to 7 or any contravention of section 8; or

(b) as affecting the extent (if any) to which breach of a duty imposed by any of the existing statutory provisions is actionable; or

*(c) as affecting the operation of section 12 of the **M14**Nuclear Installations Act 1965 (right to compensation by virtue of certain provisions of that Act).*

*(2) Breach of a duty imposed by health and safety regulations **F132**. . . shall, so far as it causes damage, be actionable except in so far as the regulations provide otherwise.*

*(3) No provision made by virtue of section 15(6)(b) shall afford a defence in any civil proceedings, whether brought by virtue of subsection (2) above or not; but as regards any duty imposed as mentioned in subsection (2) above health and safety regulations **F132**. . . may provide for any defence specified in the regulations to be available in any action for breach of that duty.*

(4) Subsections (1)(a) and (2) above are without prejudice to any right of action which exists apart from the provisions of this Act, and subsection (3) above is without prejudice to any defence which may be available apart from the provisions of the regulations there mentioned.

*(5) Any term of an agreement which purports to exclude or restrict the operation of subsection (2) above, or any liability arising by virtue of that subsection shall be void, except in so far as health and safety regulations **F132**. . . provide otherwise.*

(6) In this section "damage" includes the death of, or injury to, any person (including any disease and any impairment of a person's physical or mental condition).

Thus it was going all the way back to 1974, that statutory duties were imposed upon employers that imposed civil liabilities for breaches of the various employment Regulations, which will be dealt with separately in this book. This has arguably been a policy decision of a Conservative Government, to reduce the burden of compensation claims upon employers.

How will the changes to Section 69 work in practice?

Section 69 of the Regulatory Reform Act is going to have a number of important changes for those handling Employers' Liability Claims. For example:-

(a) It is important to remember that the duties imposed by the various Regulations will still apply. Indeed the Courts when determining whether that has been a breach of the common law duty of care will likely still look to the Regulations to what duties the Regulations impose upon an employer. However, a breach of a Regulation itself will not impose civil liability.

(b) In order for a Claimant to prove a claim in common law negligence, the risk must have been reasonably foreseeable. The number of claims that would previously have succeeded under strict liability under the Regulations, prior to section 69, especially claims under PUWER, may now be reduced for risks that were not foreseeable. This is discussed in more detail but it is prudent to say here that at common law, the overall test for negligence is that of *the reasonable and prudent employer taking positive thought for the safety of his workers in light of what he knows or ought to know.' (Stokes v Guest (1968) 1WLR 1886).* This will be discussed in more detail in other chapters.

(c) The changes undoubtedly mean that it will be more difficult for Claimants to succeed in EL claims. The changes mean that it is more important than ever for the Claimant's Solicitor to consider whether common law breach of a duty of care is likely to be established, and if it cannot be, close the claim, as it will fail at Trial.

(d) It is important to remember that even though breach of the Regulations imposes strict liability, it will still be important to consider the Regulations and plead the Regulations in the Particulars of Claim, as guidance to the likely standard of duty to be applied by the Court at Trial. All too often all the Regulations are pleaded in either the Claim Notification Form or the Particulars of Claim, or not at all. It is important to consider, which Regulations are likely to apply and why, to the Particular factors of a case. All the Regulations are considered in detail in other chapters.

(e) It is very important to remember that the Regulations only apply to accidents occurring on or after 1 October 2013. Although the old cases are now running out, it is important to note that in any case, where the date of the accident is before 1 October 2013, some Regulations still impose strict liability and breach of some Regulations impose civil liability, so it is essential that these are still pleaded in the Particulars of Claim, where appropriate.

(f) It may be argued that there will be an increased need for expert evidence in areas such as engineering as Claimants try to meet the requirement of showing what happened and why it was negligent. The provision of engineering evidence in various types of accidents will be discussed in other chapters and this will be an area this book will look at in detail.

Section 69: A Case in Point – Reasonable Foreseeability v Breach of Statutory Duty

An example of this can be found in *HIDE v STEEPLECHASE CO (CHELTENHAM) LTD & ORS (2013)[2013] EWCA Civ 545.*

The facts are as follows:-

1. *He was riding a horse called "Hatch a Plan". The race was 2 miles in length and included several hurdles. A guard rail about 4 feet high ran around the outside of the track primarily to contain loose horses. A rail also ran intermittently on the inside of the track. Due to their intended purpose, the rails were built to be quite strong; they were made of PVC or some plastic material and secured into the ground by upright posts also of plastic on top of metal spigots. The upright posts were padded for 20 to 25 yards following each hurdle. Mr Linley, the Senior Inspector of Courses for the British Horseracing Authority, gave evidence that the padding was 2 to 3 centimetres thick.*

2. *The first of the hurdles was located approximately 100 yards from the start. It was 20 yards wide and set up towards the outside of the track; there was a distance of approximately 4 feet between the outside edge of the hurdle and the guard rail. The hurdle itself was described as being "fairly modest". The total width of the track where the hurdle was positioned was 46 yards.*

3. *During the race, Mr Hide jumped over the hurdle towards its right hand side approximately 13 feet 6 inches (or 4 and a half yards) from the outside guard rail. After clearing the hurdle, his horse stumbled and fell. The horse careered sharply to the right, which caused Mr Hide to fall from his mount; he hit the ground and then moved (at speed) side ways or backwards into contact with one of the guard rail upright posts hitting it with his left hip. The judge found that it was a very unusual type of fall which would not have been expected or reasonably foreseen. Mr Hide sustained a fractured pelvis and a head injury. Happily he has made a good recovery. Damages have been agreed at £58,000 if the defendant is liable.*

4. *In an action which was not commenced until 9th November 2009, and regrettably not brought to trial until June 2012, Mr Hide sought damages against the management of the racecourse. Three bodies were joined. The second defendant, Jockey Club Racecourses Limited, is the correct defendant and nothing turns on the joinder of the other two defendants.*

5. *Mr Hide relied largely upon regulation 4 of the Provision and Use of Work Equipment Regulations 1998 ("the Regulations") which provided that work equipment is to be so constructed or adapted as to be suitable for the purpose for which it is provided.*

The Trial Judge's conclusion on the facts:-

11. *Having set out the relevant terms of the Regulations he then reached the following conclusions:- (1) both the railings and the hurdles were work equipment from the point of view of the employees who put them up; (2) Mr Hide used the hurdle but not the railings; (3)*

there was nothing wrong with the hurdle; (4) the railing was a suitable railing; (5) Mr Hide had not established that the padding was unsuitable; and (6) **the relative disposition of the hurdle and the railing did not make either of them unsuitable for the purpose for which they were used or provided.**

However, the Judge then went onto infer a test of reasonable foreseeability into the Regulations where he said:-

He described the question whether the relative disposition of the hurdle and railing rendered them unsuitable for the purpose for which they were used or provided as lying at the heart of the case and said this at his point of decision:-

"51.   The answer must I think be found in the phrases "suitable for the purpose for which it is used or provided" and "reasonably foreseeable". The purpose of a racing obstacle is to provide a test of nerve and skill for horse and rider and thus a pleasure for the spectator, not to mention profit for the betting industry. In deciding what is a suitable jump or course layout, a course designer can and should bear in mind what is reasonably likely to happen. Is there a reasonably foreseeable source of harm? This must be a matter of judgment and degree. If a jump was so dangerous as to make injury probable, as opposed to merely foreseeable, then it would, strongly arguably, be unsuitable within the meaning of the regulation.

52.   The concept of reasonable foreseeability, a classic common law phrase, is imported in regulation 4. This, in my judgment, enables the manager of a racecourse appropriately to consider not whether a layout is a conceivable or "foreseeable" cause of injury, but whether the injury is "reasonably foreseeable", viz whether the injury is likely or unlikely in the circumstances. If in the view of those with knowledge and experience of racing a layout is not thought likely to be a cause of danger, then it is likely to be "suitable". It might also be observed that regulation 4(4) uses the expression suitable in any respect which it is reasonably foreseeable "will", not "may", affect health and safety. It must be harder to establish that a state of affairs will affect safety than that it may.

53.   *This racecourse was, I find, administered by experienced and conscientious people who were alive to safety issues. They did "have regard to the working conditions and to the risks of safety" which existed (regulation 4(2)). Their intention was, as was the purpose of the regulations, "to promote a culture of good practice with a view to preventing injury" (per Lord Hope in Smith supra at paragraph 15). The course was invigilated by an inspectorate with similar qualities. Mr Hide called them good people. The hurdle and rails were erected under the hand and eye of a suitably experienced and knowledgeable groundsman who understood the behaviour of horse and rider. It was used by experienced jockeys, always alive to the risks of falling from or with their horses. The jockeys have safety representatives.*

54.   *The considerations which the organisers and their staff gave to the arrangements was, I am satisfied, at least as efficacious as a formal risk assessment as envisaged by the regulations, which may or may not have taken place. I have no doubt that the views of these people alone and in combination, were and are the best indication of what disposition of hurdle and fence was "suitable", including suitable in respects in which it was reasonably foreseeable would affect the safety of any person. All had safety in mind when fulfilling their respective roles and all had a good understanding of what was likely and unlikely to happen. None thought that an accident of this kind was at all likely, though of course it was possible, and in that sense foreseeable. None had any doubts about the suitability of the arrangements at the material time."*

12.   *As I read the above paragraphs the judge is applying the phrase "reasonably foreseeable" as a common lawyer would in resolving a case of negligence and then says that the layout of the hurdle and the rail is likely to be suitable "if in the view of those with knowledge and experience of racing a layout is not thought likely to be a cause of danger."*

> *The question is whether the judge was correct to use the concept of reasonable forseeability in the classic common law manner when assessing liability under the regulations. It might also be a question whether the judge's use of the word "likely" unacceptably dilutes the concept of reasonable foreseeability in any event. A yet further question is whether the views of the organisers of the racecourse and their staff can truly be "the best indication of what disposition of hurdle and fence was "suitable"" as the judge states in paragraph 54, even though the judge accepted that an accident of the kind that occurred was possible "and in that sense foreseeable"*

However the Court found the judge had erred in importing the common law phrase of "reasonable foreseeability" into the PUWER when deciding whether a perimeter rail at a racecourse was suitable work equipment. Once a Claimant had shown that he had suffered injury as a result of contact with a piece of work equipment which might be unsuitable, it was for the Defendant to show that the accident was due to unforeseeable circumstances beyond his control, or to exceptional events, the consequences of which were unavoidable despite the exercise of all due care on his part.

The Court said:-

> *Once, therefore, the claimant shows that he has suffered injury as a result of contact with a piece of work equipment which is (or may be) unsuitable, it will be for the defendant to show that the accident was due to unforeseeable circumstances beyond his control or to exceptional events the consequences of which could not be avoided in spite of the exercise of all due care on his part. The fact that an injury occurs in an unexpected way will not excuse the defendant unless he can show further that the circumstances were "unforeseeable" or "exceptional" in the sense given to those words by the Directive.*

> *26. It follows from all this that the judge was, with respect, incorrect to import into Regulation 4 the "classic common law phrase" of "reas-*

onable foreseeability" and then dismiss the claim on the basis (1) that the way in which Mr Hide was injured was very unusual and (2) that the defendant had abided by all the requirements of the BHA and could not be expected to do more. Those factors might once have excused a defendant in a case brought at common law (although the relevance of the first factor may even then be questionable in the light of Hughes v Lord Advocate [1963] AC 837) but the Directives and therefore the Regulations exist in a world different from the common law. Adapting the words of Lord Rodger in Robb the primary purpose of the relevant regulations is to ensure that employers (and other defendants) take the necessary steps to prevent foreseeable harm coming to their employees in the first place and the defendant's obligations are triggered if it is reasonably foreseeable that an employee might injure himself. As the judge himself said (para 54) an accident of the kind that happened to Mr Hide, while not at all likely, was possible and in that sense foreseeable. If it happens, it will be for the defendant to show that it was due to unforeseeable circumstances beyond his control or to exceptional events the consequences of which could not be avoided.

27. *This the defendant cannot do. Quite apart from the fact that the defendant did not plead any such unforeseeable circumstances or exceptional events (which is perhaps understandable since the potential difficulties raised by the transposition of Directives into the Regulation only emerged fully in the supplemental skeleton filed on behalf of Mr Hide shortly before the hearing), it is difficult to see what unforeseeable circumstances or exceptional events could be relied on. I do not myself see that an unusual fall could be classified as either. Even if it could, the circumstances of that fall cannot be said to be beyond the control of the defendant or to have engendered events which could not be avoided despite the exercise of all due care. The padding of the uprights of the guard rail could have been thicker; the hurdle could have been placed at a greater distance from the guard rail. The defendants cannot show that if either or both precautions had been taken, Mr Hide would inevitably have suffered the injury which he did. I should perhaps add that not only the hurdle but also the guard rail were, in my view, being "used" as*

> *"work equipment". The fact that Mr Hide did not expect to come into contact with the guard rail does not mean that he was not using the guard rail"*

Thus in *Hide,* which was a pre section 69 ERRA case, the Court found on Appeal for the Defendant, by applying the strict liability test under PUWER. However, if there were a post section 69 EERA case, the situation may have been different given strict liability would no longer apply, and the reasonable foreseeability test would be correct. The Court said:-

> 28. *"It is true that a breach of the Regulations can give rise to criminal liability. But the Regulation is to be regarded as giving rise to a form of liability which is a stricter liability than at common law. It would be wrong to dilute the liability aspect of the Regulations when questions of the degree of fault can always be taken into account in sentencing"*

It is now of course the case that had this accident happened on or after 1 October 2013, the test implied in this case would have been one of reasonable foreseeability, and the Claimant may not have succeeded, as he could not have relied upon section 4 of PUWER in respect of strict liability.

Employer's Liability (Defective Equipment) Act 1969

This Act is not amended by section 69 of ERRA and sets out:-

> *Extension of employer's liability for defective equipment.*
> *(1) Where after the commencement of this Act—*
> *(a) an employee suffers personal injury in the course of his employment in consequence of a defect in equipment provided by his employer for the purposes of the employer's business; and*
> *(b) the defect is attributable wholly or partly to the fault of a third party (whether identified or not),*
> *the injury shall be deemed to be also attributable to negligence on the part of the employer (whether or not he is liable in respect of the*

injury apart from this subsection), but without prejudice to the law relating to contributory negligence and to any remedy by way of contribution or in contract or otherwise which is available to the employer in respect of the injury.

(2) In so far as any agreement purports to exclude or limit any liability of an employer arising under subsection (1) of this section, the agreement shall be void.

(3) In this section—

"business" includes the activities carried on by any public body;

"employee" means a person who is employed by another person under a contract of service or apprenticeship and is so employed for the purposes of a business carried on by that other person, and "employer" shall be construed accordingly;

"equipment" includes any plant and machinery, vehicle, aircraft and clothing;

"fault" means negligence, breach of statutory duty or other act or omission which gives rise to liability in tort in England and Wales or which is wrongful and gives rise to liability in damages in Scotland; and

"personal injury" includes loss of life, any impairment of a person's physical or mental condition and any disease.

(4) This section binds the Crown, and persons in the service of the Crown shall accordingly be treated for the purposes of this section as employees of the Crown if they would not be so treated apart from this subsection.

The Act arguably has not been used in work equipment cases since 1992, given the use of PUWER, but may be a useful pleading in case of negligence for defective Work Equipment cases, where the accident happens on or after 1 October 2013.

Conclusions

There is no doubt that section 69 of the ERRA, will create difficulties for Claimant Solicitors, especially with reference to work equipment cases, under PUWER, which for accidents before 1 October 2013, imposed strict liability. There will undoubtedly be further arguments before the Courts as to how the interplay between the Regulations as evidence of negligence is played out. Claimant Lawyers will now have to be more careful than ever to show there has been a breach of duty of the common law duty of care and that breach caused the accident. This will be discussed in more detail in other chapters.

CHAPTER FIVE
CAUSATION INVESTIGATIONS:
MEDICAL CAUSATION ISSUES,
GATHERING MEDICAL RECORDS
AND CREDIBILITY ISSUES

Causation is one of the most important aspects when considering any Employers' Liability Claim. The reason of course for this is that even if the Claimant can succeed on the issue of breach of duty, the Claimant still has to prove causation in relation to the injuries sustained. This becomes even more important when the credibility of the Claimant is at issue between the parties.

The Claimant of course will have to prove legal and medical causation on the balance of probability. Establishing causation at an early stage in the case will be as important as establishing breach of duty given that if the Claimant's case fails on the issues of causation, there is little point in establishing breach of duty in the first instance.

This chapter will therefore concentrate solely on investigating causation in relation to Employer's Liability Claims and focus on the early investigations to be undertaken in relation to such cases at the outset.

Early Investigation

Early investigation of causation is always going to be key in relation to an Employers' Liability case. This will be particularly important if the Defendant puts the Claimant on notice that causation is going to be an issue.

This inevitably leads to the question as to how causation can be investigated in relation to such a case at an early stage and how can it be investigated economically, particularly with reference to fixed costs and portal costs that have been discussed in chapters one and two of this book.

The issue of causation can be investigated economically in the following ways:-

Medical Causation

a) The Claimant's Solicitor will wish to obtain the Claimant's General Practitioner records and hospital records at the first opportunity. The Claimant's solicitor should carefully go through the Claimant's contemporaneous GP and hospital records as this will often provide clues as to the mechanism of the accident.

b) The Claimant's Solicitor will also likely wish to obtain a copy of the accident report form, HSE reports and any witness evidence to check if the mechanism of the accident is consistent with how the Claimant says it occurred.

c) If there is any variation in the notes, careful instructions will need to be taken from the Claimant as to the reason for any inconsis-tencies and some of the following are some possible examples from practice:-

 i.   The claimant says that they have tripped over a hole in the employer's car park, yet the medical records suggest they fell at home.
 ii. The Claimant says they suffered a laceration from a piece of machinery at work, yet the hospital notes suggest the injury was sustained in a nightclub.

One has to bear in mind that sometimes the treating medical practi-tioner in a rush at the Accident & Emergency Department or the hospital doctor may get it wrong in the heat of the moment but the Claimant's Lawyer should be particularly cautious if the mechanism of the accident described has been described incorrectly to both the GP and the treating doctor in the Accident & Emergency Department. If there are any inconsistencies in contemporaneous medical records, the Claimant's solicitor can sometimes seek to interview the treating GP or hospital doctor in order to confirm if there is any explanation for the notes being incorrect.

Consider the mechanism of the claimant's fall if there are inconsistencies between the GP and the hospital notes. For example, if the claimant states that they tripped over on their right foot in the accident report form but the medical records suggest that the claimant had tripped up on their left foot and these are recorded contemporaneously post-accident this should give rise to caution. It is of course the case that sometimes there are credible explanations for inconsistencies but in the writer's experience, the Courts tend to treat contemporaneous medical records as having a degree of credibility given that they are recorded shortly after the accident and often before it is known that a claim is being made. This is also true of accident report forms, if they were checked and signed by the Claimant.

It may be argued that it is often very difficult for a Claimant Lawyer to get over serious inconsistencies as to the recording of the mechanism of the accident, without any supporting evidence in respect of the same. If someone has slipped or tripped on an employer's premises and broken their ankle, and there are clear photographs of the defect, this of course does not automatically mean that the Claimant has slipped as suggested and it is always possible that the injury could have been caused elsewhere.

Some commentators have argued that fraud in this area is on the increase given the tightening of the insurer's investigations into whiplash type fraud, and Claimant Lawyers need to be very careful it may be argued to ensure that the Claimant's evidence is credible in relation to the mechanism of the accident.

Recording The Accident Circumstances – The Contemporaneous Version of Events

It is extremely important that the Claimant's Solicitor obtains from the outset an extremely detailed version of events from the Claimant to the mechanism of the accident, and exactly how the injury was sustained, that can be tested later to test the credibility of the first version of events given by the Claimant.

Arguably, this is even more important now since the first version given by the Claimant, recorded in the Claim Notification Form has to be verified by a Statement of truth.

It is important that the Claim Notification Form version of events gives enough information to the Defendant to investigate the claim at the outset, and some of the following information and questions may be useful when taking instructions from the Claimant on an Employers' Liability Claim at the outset:-

1. Where exactly did the accident happen?

2. What was the date and time of the accident?

3. Exactly how did the accident happen?

4. Was the Claimant instructed to undertake the task in question, and if so, by whom and when?

5. Why does the Claimant believe the employer was at fault for the accident?

6. Were there any witnesses to the accident? Will the witnesses co-operate?

7. Was the Claimant wearing any protective work equipment (PPE)?

8. If not, should PPE have been provided and if so, what PPE items should have been provided?

9. Was the Claimant using work equipment at the time of the accident?

10. Was there a fault with the work equipment and if so, exactly what was the fault?

11. Has the work equipment been maintained and if so, how and when was it last serviced?

12. Did the work equipment have any warnings and if so, where were they positioned and what did they say?

13. If the accident was caused by work equipment, was there a safety guard/safety features on the equipment, and if so, were these being utilised when the accident happened?

14. Was the Claimant trained to undertake the work and if so, what training had been provided and when?

15. Was there a risk assessment in relation to the task and if so, when was the training provided?

16. Had the Claimant asked for assistance with the task before and if so, from who and when?

17. Had the Claimant been given a warning not to undertake the task, and if so, from who and when?

18. Has the employer changed procedures since the accident and if so, how and when?

Causation – The Common Themes

When one is investigating an Employer's Liability Claim, common themes often arise in terms of the issue of causation and whether the breach of duty contributed to the injuries sustained. Some of these may be broadly defined as follows:-

a) In a slip/trip claim in the workplace - was the Claimant running or walking at the time of the accident? It is common sense that lots of accidents are caused through people running rather than walking. At the outset of the claim detailed questions should be taken from the Claimant as to whether they were running or walking when the accident took place. If the Claimant was running when the accident took place, careful consideration should be given to possible findings of contributory negligence.

b) Had the Claimant consumed alcohol and if so, how much and when? This question will be particularly relevant if the Claimant had consumed a lot of alcohol in close proximity to the accident time or if this is present in the GP/Hospital records. It may be argued that Claimant Lawyers should be particularly wary of Claimants who have consumed a large amount of alcohol prior to an accident, as this may sound in contributory negligence, if not to extinguish any finding of liability on behalf of the Defendant entirely if the Claimant was severely intoxicated at the time of the accident.

In order to investigate the issues, careful instructions should be taken from the Claimant as to how much alcohol had been con-sumed prior to the accident and in particular, one should look at the hospital and GP notes for any contemporaneous records as to whether the claimant had been drinking or not prior to the accident.

c) Did the Claimant trip in the workplace? In terms of the credibility of tripping claims, one needs to ask the Claimant carefully, at the outset of the claim, how the tripping incident occurred. For example, did the Claimant trip with the left or the right foot, did the foot go entirely into the hole and what caused the Claimant to trip, did the Claimant's foot get caught on the edge of the defect, and in which direction did the Claimant fall?

Does the Claimant's version of events make sense in terms of the mechanism of the tripping claim? For example, if the Claimant's foot gets caught on the edge of a defect, they are likely to fall for-wards and not sideways. Whereas, if the Claimant puts their foot in an open manhole cover, they are likely to fall to the side, given their entire body weight will have been taken away from them and they will fall towards the side by which the foot has fallen into the manhole cover. When looking at the Claimant's version of events, ask yourself does it make sense?

d) Was this a slipping incident? If the Claimant has slipped, if someone slips, it may be argued that one generally would expect the witnesses evidence to be that their foot had gone from underneath them, and a witness will usually describe a lack of grip under foot or similar prior to the fall and they may describe "their feet going from underneath them".

e) It is always important to establish which foot the Claimant slipped on. Was it the Claimant's left foot or their right foot and again is their version of events credible with regards to the way that they fell and the way that they landed following the fall?

The Claimant is the Author of his own Misfortune

A difficulty with many Employer's Liability cases, is that all too often, employees left to their own devices at work sometimes contribute to their own accidents. Contributory negligence has been dealt with in detail in other chapters but in the context of Employer's Liability Claims, it is always essential to look at whether the Claimant has in fact exercised reasonable care for his own safety and if there is a degree of contributory negligence (as there often is in many EL claims) to consider early Part 36 offers to take account of this, especially when dealing with claims within a fixed costs regime.

Summary

Therefore, when assessing claims at the outset, it is important that the Claimant's lawyer looks at all the potential contributory factors to an accident when looking at the issue of causation.

Given that the Claim Notification Form is now verified with a Statement of Truth, it is essential that detailed instructions are taken from the Claimant at the outset of the claim as to the mechanism of the accident and the way in which it was caused and if there are any inconsistencies or any concerns the claimant's general practitioner and hospital records, together with the accident report form and witnesses evidence are obtained at the first opportunity in order to check the consistency of events.

Post-Jackson and in fixed costs unless there are credible explanations for inconsistencies, the Claimant's Lawyer may well be wary of progressing claims that fall outside the portal in fixed costs where there are such serious inconsistencies.

The Claimant's Solicitor must also ensure that the version provided to the GP or Orthopedic Surgeon is detailed and that the Claimant's Lawyer should check the consistency of the version given to the Claimant's medical expert, as compared to the version that was given to the Claimant's Lawyer at the outset of the case and any inconsistencies in this are addressed urgently at the outset of the case.

It may be argued that there is little room within a fixed costs regime to run cases where there are serious inconsistencies as to legal or medical causation between the version of events in the Claim Notification Form, the GP records, the Accident and Emergency notes, and the version that is given to the Claimant's medical expert.

If there are serious inconsistencies in the version of events provided which lack explanation, the Claimant's lawyer may at this stage, give some serious consideration as to whether it is a claim that should be litigated.

CHAPTER SIX
SLIPS AND TRIPS IN THE WORKPLACE: TRAFFIC ROUTE REGULATIONS, NEGLIGENCE, LIABILITY INVESTIGATIONS, AND ACCIDENTS RELATED TO LIFTS, VEHICLES AND ESCALATORS

There are a number of relevant Regulations that can be pleaded and utilised in pre section 69 ERRA cases (see earlier chapters regarding the Enterprise Act).

The Workplace (Health, Safety and Welfare Regulations 1992), came into effect on 1 January 1996, for all workplaces. The relevant Regulations for slip and trip cases in the workplace are set out as follows. The relevance of each of the Regulations is discussed in the following paragraphs:-

Maintenance of workplace, and of equipment, devices and systems

5.—(1) The workplace and the equipment, devices and systems to which this regulation applies shall be maintained (including cleaned as appropriate) in an efficient state, in efficient working order and in good repair.

Lighting
8.—(1) Every workplace shall have suitable and sufficient lighting.
(2) The lighting mentioned in paragraph (1) shall, so far as is reasonably practicable, be by natural light.
(3) Without prejudice to the generality of paragraph (1), suitable and sufficient emergency lighting shall be provided in any room in circumstances in which persons at work are specially exposed to danger in the event of failure of artificial lighting.

Cleanliness and waste materials

9.—*(1) Every workplace and the furniture, furnishings and fittings therein shall be kept sufficiently clean.*

(2) The surfaces of the floors, walls and ceilings of all workplaces inside buildings shall be capable of being kept sufficiently clean.

(3) So far as is reasonably practicable, waste materials shall not be allowed to accumulate in a workplace except in suitable receptacles.

Room dimensions and space

10.—*(1) Every room where persons work shall have sufficient floor area, height and unoccupied space for purposes of health, safety and welfare.*

Condition of floors and traffic routes

12.—*(1) Every floor in a workplace and the surface of every traffic route in a workplace shall be of a construction such that the floor or surface of the traffic route is suitable for the purpose for which it is used.*

(2) Without prejudice to the generality of paragraph (1), the requirements in that paragraph shall include requirements that—

(a) the floor, or surface of the traffic route, shall have no hole or slope, or be uneven or slippery so as, in each case, to expose any person to a risk to his health or safety; and

(b) every such floor shall have effective means of drainage where necessary.

(3) So far as is reasonably practicable, every floor in a workplace and the surface of every traffic route in a workplace shall be kept free from obstructions and from any article or substance which may cause a person to slip, trip or fall.

(4) In considering whether for the purposes of paragraph (2)(a) a hole or slope exposes any person to a risk to his health or safety—

(a) no account shall be taken of a hole where adequate measures have been taken to prevent a person falling; and

(b) account shall be taken of any handrail provided in connection with any slope.

(5) Suitable and sufficient handrails and, if appropriate, guards shall be provided on all traffic routes which are staircases except in circum-

stances in which a handrail can not be provided without obstructing the traffic route.

Organisation etc. of traffic routes

17.—(1) Every workplace shall be organised in such a way that pedestrians and vehicles can circulate in a safe manner.

(2) Traffic routes in a workplace shall be suitable for the persons or vehicles using them, sufficient in number, in suitable positions and of sufficient size.

(3) Without prejudice to the generality of paragraph (2), traffic routes shall not satisfy the requirements of that paragraph unless suitable measures are taken to ensure that—

(a) pedestrians or, as the case may be, vehicles may use a traffic route without causing danger to the health or safety of persons at work near it;

(b) there is sufficient separation of any traffic route for vehicles from doors or gates or from traffic routes for pedestrians which lead onto it; and

(c) where vehicles and pedestrians use the same traffic route, there is sufficient separation between them.

(4) All traffic routes shall be suitably indicated where necessary for reasons of health or safety.

(5) Paragraph (2) shall apply so far as is reasonably practicable, to a workplace which is not a new workplace, a modification, an extension or a conversion.

A useful document to consider in conjunction with the Workplace Regulations is the accompanying code of Practice which sets out:-

"Although failure to comply with any provision of the ACOP is not in itself an offence, the failure may be taken by a Court in criminal proceedings as proof that a person has contravened the regulation to which the provision relates. In such a case, however, it will be open to that person to satisfy the Court that he or she has complied with the regulation in some other way".

The code of practice in the context of slip and trips claims, the following useful guidance, regarding duties of employers generally may serve as a useful reminder as to who has responsibility under the Regulations:-

Duties under these Regulations
4 People other than employers also have duties under these Regulations if they have control, to any extent, of a workplace. For example, owners, landlords or managing agents of business premises should ensure that common parts, common facilities, common services and means of access within their control comply with the Regulations.

5 Their duties are limited to matters which are within their control. For example, an owner who is responsible for the general condition of a lobby, staircase and landings, for shared toilets provided for tenants' use, and for maintaining ventilation plant, should ensure that those parts and plant comply with these Regulations. However, the owner is not responsible under these Regulations for matters outside their control, for example a spillage caused by a tenant or shortcomings in the day- to-day cleaning of sanitary facilities where this is the tenants' responsibility. Tenants should co-operate sufficiently with each other, and with the landlord, to ensure that the requirements of the Regulations are fully met.

Walkways, Lifts and Moving Walkways

Sometimes one may find a slip, trip or fall in the workplace is caused as a consequence of for example an escalator, lift doors or moving walkways. The guidance in the ACOP makes it clear that under Regulation 5, these matters are required to have a system of maintenance as follows under Regulation 5:-

41 The systems mentioned in these Regulations should be free of faults likely to affect the health, safety or welfare of workers and provide an adequate level of hygiene. If a potentially dangerous defect is discovered, the defect should be rectified immediately or steps should be taken to protect anyone who might be put at risk.

42 Equipment that could fail and put workers at serious risk should be properly maintained and checked at regular intervals, as appropriate, by inspection, testing, adjustment, lubrication, repair and cleaning.

43 Any faults should be properly rectified as soon as possible. Action should be taken immediately to isolate and rectify the fault where there is a risk of serious or imminent harm. Where the defect does not pose a danger but makes the equipment unsuitable for use, for example a broken toilet, it may be taken out of service until it is repaired or replaced. However, if this would result in the number of facilities being fewer than the minimum set out in Tables 1 and 2 on page 39 the defect should be rectified without delay.

44 The frequency of regular maintenance, and precisely what it involves and who is competent to complete it, will depend on the equipment or device concerned. There is guidance from HSE9,10 and you can get advice from other authoritative sources, particularly manufacturers' information and instructions, as well as relevant trade literature.

45 Advice on systems of maintenance for buildings can be found in publications by the Chartered Institution of Building Services Engineers (CIBSE).11 The maintenance of work equipment, personal protective equipment, and electrical systems, equipment and conductors, is addressed in other Regulations and relevant guidance.9,12-15 HSE's website has advice on operating escalators16 and there are British Standards covering escalators17 and window access equipment18. An 'efficient state' means that the workplace and the equipment.

46 Examples of equipment and devices which require a system of maintenance include:
- *emergency lighting;*
- *fencing;*
- *fixed equipment used for window cleaning;*
- *anchorage points for safety harnesses;*
- *devices to limit the opening of windows;*

- *powered doors;*
- *escalators;*
- *moving walkways.*

Lighting

Sometimes in the context of slip and trip claims, one can find lighting (or lack of it) can contribute to an accident. ACOP assists as follows:-

81 Lighting should be sufficient to enable people to work, use facilities without experiencing eye-strain, and safely move from place to place.

82 Where necessary, artificial lighting should be provided at individual workstations, and at places of particular risk such as pedestrian crossing points on traffic routes. Stairs should be kept well lit and the lighting should not cast shadows over the main part of the treads. Outdoor traffic routes used by pedestrians should be adequately lit after dark.

83 Lights and light fittings must be selected, positioned and maintained, so that they avoid annoying glare and do not cause a hazard (eg electrical, fire, radiation or collision).

84 Lights and windows should be cleaned, repaired or replaced, as necessary, before the level of lighting becomes insufficient. Avoid obscuring light by placing items in front of lights and windows (eg stacked goods). Light switches should be positioned so that they may be found and used easily and without risk.

Cleaning and Suitability of Floors

Sometimes a floor that had not been mopped or cleaned properly can be the cause of an accident. The ACOP guidelines set out the following:-

90 Sufficiently clean means that workplaces should be regularly cleaned to ensure that dirt or refuse is not allowed to accumulate and spillages and deposits are removed or cleaned up as soon as possible. The fre-

quency of this activity and standard of cleanliness will depend on the nature of the business.

91 The surfaces of floors, walls and ceilings should be maintained, treated and repaired so they can be cleaned properly.

92 Cleaning should be carried out by an effective and suitable method and without creating, or exposing anyone to, a health or safety risk.

94 Absorbent floors, such as untreated concrete or timber, which are likely to be contaminated by oil or other substances that are difficult to remove, should preferably be sealed or coated, for example with a suitable non-slip floor paint. Carpets should also be avoided in such situations.

Condition of Floors and Traffic Routes

In terms of slipping and tripping claims this is probably the most important Regulation. ACOP sets out the general guidance that employers should adopt:-

108 Floor and traffic routes should be of sound construction and should have adequate strength and stability, taking account of the loads placed on them and the traffic passing over them. Floors should not be over-loaded.

109 The surfaces of floors and traffic routes should be free from any hole, slope, or uneven or slippery surface which is likely to cause:

- *a person to slip, trip or fall;*
- *a person to drop or lose control of anything being lifted or carried;*
- *instability or loss of control of vehicles and/or their loads.*

110 Damaged surfaces that may cause a person to trip or fall should be made good and conspicuously marked or protected until this can be done. Temporary holes should be adequately guarded. Take account of people with disabilities. Surfaces with small holes (for example metal gratings) are acceptable provided they are not likely to be a hazard. For deep holes where there is a risk of a fall, you should refer to regulation 13 and associated ACOP text, and the Work at Height Regulations 2005.

111 Slopes should not be steeper than necessary. Moderate and steep slopes, and ramps used by people with disabilities, should have a secure handrail where necessary.

112 Surfaces of floors and traffic routes likely to get wet, or to be subject to spillages, should be of a type which does not become unduly slippery. Floors near hazards that could cause injury if anyone were to fall against them (for example a woodworking or grinding machine) should be slip-resistant and be kept free from slippery substances or loose materials.

113 Where a leak, spillage or other type of contamination occurs and is likely to be a slipping hazard, take immediate steps to fence it off, clean it up, or cover it with something to stop it being slippery (eg absorbent granules).

114 Where a floor is liable to be made wet through work activity, drains and channels should be provided and positioned to minimise the area of wet floor, and the floor should slope slightly towards the drain. Where necessary to prevent tripping hazards, ensure drains and channels have covers which should be as near flush as possible with the floor surface.

115 Where reasonably practicable, processes and plant that may discharge or leak liquids should be enclosed (for example by bunding), and leaks from taps or discharge points on pipes, drums and tanks should be caught or drained away. Stop valves should be fitted to filling points on tank-filling lines. Where work involves carrying or handling liquids or slippery substances, as in food processing and preparation, the workplace and work surfaces should be arranged to minimise the likelihood of spillages.

116 Arrangements should be made to minimise risks from snow and ice. This may involve gritting, snow clearing and closure of some routes, particularly outside stairs, ladders and walkways on roofs.

117 Floors and traffic routes should be kept free of obstructions that may present a hazard or impede access. This is particularly important in any place where an obstruction is likely to cause an accident, for example near emergency routes, stairs, corners or junctions.

118 Where a temporary obstruction is unavoidable and is likely to be a hazard, prevent access or take steps to warn people (including drivers) by, for example, the use of hazard cones. Vehicles should not be parked where they are likely to be a hazard. Materials that fall onto traffic routes should be cleared as soon as possible.

119 Every open side of a staircase should be securely fenced. As a minimum, the fencing should consist of an upper rail at 900 mm or higher, and a lower rail.

120 A secure and substantial handrail should be provided and maintained on at least one side of every staircase, except at points where a handrail would obstruct entry or exit, such as steps in a theatre aisle. Handrails should be provided on both sides if there is a particular risk of falling, for example where stairs are heavily used, or are wide, have narrow treads, or where there are liable to be spillages on them. Additional handrails should be provided down the centre of particularly wide staircases where necessary.

121 A traffic route means a route for pedestrian traffic, vehicles or both and includes any stairs, staircase, fixed ladder, doorway, gateway, loading bay or ramp.

122 Slips and trips are the most common cause of injury at work. Most slips occur when floors become wet or contaminated and many trips are due to poor housekeeping.

123 To prevent slips and trips:

- *stop floors getting wet or contaminated in the first place;*
- *have effective arrangements for both routine cleaning and dealing with spills;*
- *remove spillages promptly;*
- *leave smooth floors dry after cleaning or exclude pedestrians until the floor is dry;*
- *use the right cleaning methods for your floor;*
- *look out for trip hazards (eg uneven floors, trailing cables);*
- *keep walkways and work areas clear of obstructions;*
- *encourage your workers to keep the workplace tidy;*
- *consider the use of slip-resistant flooring material.*

124 Consider providing slip-resistant footwear where slipping hazards arise despite the precautions set out in paragraph 123. Further guidance is available from HSE on slips, trips and falls (www.hse.gov.uk/slips/) and also on flooring types (www.hse.gov.uk/slips/flooring-selection-tool.htm).

125 Building Regulations have requirements on floors, stairs and ramps.1,2 Advice is available from local authorities.

126 Steep stairways are classed as fixed ladders and are dealt with under the Work at Height Regulations 2005 (www.hse.gov.uk/falls/).

Occupiers Liability Act 1957

In a slip and trip claim in the workplace there is also likely to be a claim under the Occupiers Liability Act 1957. An employer also has a duty as an Occupier to keep the area reasonably safe as follows:-

Extent of occupier's ordinary duty
(1) An occupier of premises owes the same duty, the "common duty of care", to all his visitors, except in so far as he is free to and does extend, restrict, modify or exclude his duty to any visitor or visitors by agreement or otherwise.

(2) The common duty of care is a duty to take such care as in all the circumstances of the case is reasonable to see that the visitor will be reasonably safe in using the premises for the purposes for which he is invited or permitted by the occupier to be there.

(3) The circumstances relevant for the present purpose include the degree of care, and of want of care, which would ordinarily be looked for in such a visitor, so that (for example) in proper cases—

(a) an occupier must be prepared for children to be less careful than adults; and

(b) an occupier may expect that a person, in the exercise of his calling, will appreciate and guard against any special risks ordinarily incident to it, so far as the occupier leaves him free to do so.

(4) In determining whether the occupier of premises has discharged the common duty of care to a visitor, regard is to be had to all the circumstances, so that (for example)—

(a) where damage is caused to a visitor by a danger of which he had been warned by the occupier, the warning is not to be treated without more as absolving the occupier from liability, unless in all the circumstances it was enough to enable the visitor to be reasonably safe; and

(b) where damage is caused to a visitor by a danger due to the faulty execution of any work of construction, maintenance or repair by an independent contractor employed by the occupier, the occupier is not to be treated without more as answerable for the danger if in all the circumstances he had acted reasonably in entrusting the work to an independent contractor and had taken such steps (if any) as he reasonably ought in order to satisfy himself that the contractor was competent and that the work had been properly done.

(5) The common duty of care does not impose on an occupier any obligation to a visitor in respect of risks willingly accepted as his by the visitor (the question whether a risk was so accepted to be decided on the same principles as in other cases in which one person owes a duty of care to another).

(6) For the purposes of this section, persons who enter premises for any purpose in the exercise of a right conferred by law are to be treated as permitted by the occupier to be there for that purpose, whether they in fact have his permission or not.

The key case in relation to supermarket slipping and tripping cases is *Ward –v- Tesco Stores Limited 1976 1ER 219 SCA*. In this case, the Claimant slipped on some spilled yoghurt in a supermarket and on the evidence it was established that:-

(a) The Defendant brushed the floor about half a dozen times a day.

(b) Any staff noticing a spillage were to call for its removal.

(c) Staff were to remain by the spill to guard against any accident in the interim.

The Court of Appeal held that there had not been an adequate inspection process and accordingly the Court held in the Claimant's favour.

Further discussion as to the Occupiers Liability Act 1957 is outside the scope of this book, and the reader is referred to the writer's related book entitled '*Occupiers, Highways and Defective Premises Claims: A Practical Guide Post-Jackson*'.

Slip, Trip and Fall Investigations

At the outset of the case, some of the following questions may be relevant in relation to a claim for slip/trip in the workplace may be:-

1. Where exactly did the accident happen?

2. What type of footwear was the Claimant wearing, was the Claimant carrying any items or were there any other factors which could have contributed to the accident by the Claimant?

3. How did the accident occur in the Claimant's own words?

4. Was the claimant working at the time of the accident?

5. Did the accident occur on the employer's premises?

6. What caused the Claimant to trip, fall or slip?

7. Had the Claimant seen the defect before and if so, when? Was it reported and by whom?

8. Was the defect repaired post accident and if so, when?

9. Was the accident reported and if so, when and to whom?

10. If the defect was reported, what action was taken, when and by whom?

11. Is the defect still there and if so, when did the Claimant last see it?

12. What was the size of the defect that cause the slip, trip or fall in terms of height, width and length?

13. Was the Claimant running or walking at the time of the accident?

14. Were there any witnesses to the accident?

15. Are there any witnesses who can say if the defect was present pre-accident and if so, for how long had the defect been present pre-accident?

16. Is the Claimant aware of any other similar incidents?

Accidents Involving Doors, and Other Miscellaneous Provisions

Sometimes people have accidents at work involving automatic doors or gates. Regulation 18 deals with this and sets out:-

Regulation 18 Doors and gates

(1) Doors and gates shall be suitably constructed (including being fitted with any necessary safety devices).

(2) Without prejudice to the generality of paragraph (1), doors and gates shall not comply with that paragraph unless –
(a) any sliding door or gate has a device to prevent it coming off its track during use;
(b) any upward opening door or gate has a device to prevent it falling back;
(c) any powered door or gate has suitable and effective features to prevent it causing injury by trapping any person;
(d) where necessary for reasons of health or safety, any powered door or gate can be operated manually unless it opens automatically if the power fails; and
(e) any door or gate which is capable of opening by being pushed from either side is of such a construction as to provide, when closed, a clear view of the space close to both sides.

176 Doors and gates which swing in both directions should have a transparent panel except if they are low enough to see over. Conventionally hinged doors on main traffic routes should also be fitted with such panels. Panels should be positioned so a person in a wheelchair can be seen from the other side.

177 Sliding doors should have a stop or other effective means to prevent the door coming off the track. They should also have a retaining rail to prevent the door falling should the suspension system fail or the rollers leave the track.

178 Upward opening doors should be fitted with an effective device such as a counterbalance or ratchet mechanism to prevent them falling back in a manner likely to cause injury.

179 Doors and gates should be constructed and maintained in accordance with Building Regulations,1,2 and maintained as required by regulation 5.

180 Power-operated doors and gates should have safety features to prevent people being injured as a result of being struck or trapped. Safety features include:

1. a sensitive edge, or other suitable detector, and associated trip device to stop, or reverse, the motion of the door or gate when obstructed;
2. a device to limit the closing force so that it is not enough to cause injury;
3. an operating control which must be held in position during the whole of the closing motion. This will only be suitable where the risk of injury is low and the speed of closure is slow. Such a control, when released, should cause the door to stop or reopen immediately and should be positioned so that the operator has a clear view of the door throughout its movement.

181 Where necessary, power-operated doors and gates should have a readily identifiable and accessible control switch or device so that they can be stopped quickly in an emergency. Normal on/off controls may be sufficient.

182 It should be possible to open a power-operated door or gate if the power supply fails, unless it opens automatically in such circumstances or there is an alternative way through. This does not apply to lift doors and other doors and gates which are there to prevent falls or access to areas of potential danger.

183 Where tools are necessary for manual opening they should be readily available at all times. If the power supply is restored while the door is being opened manually, the person opening it should not be put at risk.

184 When new powered doors or gates are installed, including situations where existing manually operated doors/gates are fitted with

powered actuators (whether controlled automatically or by an operator), before first use they must meet the requirements of the Supply of Machinery (Safety) Regulations 2008.34

185 Those Regulations require all machinery to be designed and constructed for safety. As well as the provision of suitable safety devices and CE marking, the machinery must be accompanied by comprehensive instructions for use and maintenance, and a Declaration of Conformity issued by the manufacturer (usually the installer of the complete product). The appropriate use of a product which complies with a European Technical Assessment, as defined in the (EU) Construction Products Regulation 305/2011, should meet the relevant requirements (http://ec.europa.eu/enterprise/sectors/construction/legislation/).

Traffic Routes, Vehicle Accidents at Work and Loading Bays

The Regulations and the APOC guidelines also usefully deal with accidents involving loading bays and persons struck by vehicles on an employer's premises as follows:-

50 'Traffic route' is defined in regulation 2 as a 'route for pedestrian traffic, vehicles or both and includes any stairs, staircase, fixed ladder, doorway, gateway, loading bay or ramp'.

151 Paragraphs 152, 158, and 162 include special provision for the management of the width and height of traffic routes in existence before 1 January 1993. These provisions reflect the requirements of regulation 17(5) that compliance with regulations 17(2) and (3) is only necessary if it is reasonably practicable to do so. This is because it might be difficult, in a few cases, for some routes in existence before the introduction of the ACOP to comply with the requirements for sufficient organisation and separation of traffic routes.

General requirements for traffic routes

152 There should be enough traffic routes, of sufficient width and headroom, to allow people on foot or in vehicles to circulate safely and without difficulty. Features that obstruct routes should be avoided. On traffic routes in existence before 1 January 1993, obstructions such as limited headroom are acceptable provided they are indicated by, for example, the use of conspicuous tape. Give special consideration to the safety of people with impaired or no sight.

153 People in wheelchairs may be at greater risk than people on foot, so give special consideration to their safety. Traffic routes used by people in wheelchairs should be wide enough to allow unimpeded access, and ramps should be provided where necessary. Regulation 12(4) and paragraph 111 of this Code also deal with ramps.

154 Access between floors should not normally be by way of ladders or steep stairs. Fixed ladders or steep stairs may be used where a conventional staircase cannot be accommodated, provided they are only used by people who are capable of using them safely and any loads can be carried safely.

155 Inadequate or unsuitable routes should not be used by vehicles. Any restrictions should be clearly indicated. Uneven or soft ground should be made smooth and firm if vehicles could overturn or shed their loads. Sharp or blind bends on vehicle routes should be avoided as far as possible. If they are unavoidable, measures such as one-way systems or using mirrors to improve vision should be considered.

156 Prominent warning should be given to limited headroom, both in advance and at the obstruction itself. Any potentially dangerous obstructions should be shielded, such as overhead electric cables or pipes containing, for example, flammable or hazardous chemicals. Screens should be provided where necessary to protect people at risk from exhaust fumes at work, or to protect people from materials likely to fall from vehicles.

157 Sensible speed limits should be set and clearly displayed on vehicle routes except those used only by slow vehicles. Where necessary, suitable speed retarders should be provided. These should always be preceded by a warning sign or a mark on the road. Forklift trucks should avoid having to pass over road humps unless the truck is of a type which can negotiate them safely.

158 Traffic routes used by vehicles should be wide enough to allow vehicles to circulate freely without having to leave the route. One-way systems or restrictions on parking should be introduced as necessary. Traffic management systems should be provided where it is not reasonably practicable to make the route wide enough for traffic routes in existence before 1 January 1993.

159 The need for vehicles with poor rear visibility to reverse should be eliminated as far as possible, for example by using one-way systems. There is further guidance on reversing in paragraph 172.

160 Traffic routes used by vehicles should not pass close to anything that is likely to collapse or be left in a dangerous state if hit (such as hollow, cast- iron columns and storage racking), or to any edge, unless they are fenced or adequately protected.

161 Where a load has to be tipped into a hopper, waste pit, or similar place, and the vehicle is liable to fall into it, provide substantial barriers or portable wheel stops at the end of the traffic route to prevent this.

Separation of people and vehicles

162 Any traffic route which is used by both pedestrians and vehicles should be wide enough to enable pedestrians to pass safely. On traffic routes in existence before 1 January 1993, where it is not reasonably practical to make the route wide enough, traffic management systems should be provided as necessary. In buildings, lines should be drawn on the floor to indicate routes followed by vehicles such as forklift trucks.

163 On routes used by automatic, driverless vehicles which are also used by pedestrians, take steps to ensure that pedestrians do not become trapped by vehicles. The vehicles should be fitted with safeguards to minimise the risk of injury and sufficient clearance provided between vehicles and pedestrians. Ensure that fixtures along the route do not create trapping hazards.

164 In doorways, gateways, tunnels, bridges, or other enclosed routes, vehicles should be separated from pedestrians by a kerb or barrier. For safety purposes, separate routes should be provided for pedestrians and they should be guided to use the correct route by clear marking. Such routes should be kept unobstructed. Similar measures should be taken where the speed or volume of vehicles would put pedestrians at risk.

165 Workstations should be adequately separated or shielded from vehicles.

Crossings

166 Appropriate crossing points should be provided and used where pedestrian and vehicle routes meet. Where necessary, barriers or rails should be provided to prevent pedestrians crossing at particularly dangerous points and to help guide them to designated crossing places. At crossing points where volumes of traffic are particularly heavy, consider providing suitable bridges or subways.

167 Where pedestrian and vehicle routes meet, there should be adequate visibility and open space. For example, where an enclosed pedestrian route (or a doorway or staircase) joins a vehicle route, there should be an open space of at least 1 m from which pedestrians can see along the vehicle route in both directions. In the case of a one-way route, the pedestrian should be able to see in the direction of oncoming traffic. Where such a space cannot be achieved, barriers or rails should be provided to prevent pedestrians walking directly onto the vehicle route.

168 **Loading bays** should have at least one exit point from the lower level. Wide loading bays should have at least two exit points, one at each end. Alternatively, a refuge should be provided which can be used to avoid being struck or crushed by a vehicle.

Signs

169 Potential hazards on traffic routes used by vehicles and people should be indicated by suitable warning signs. Such hazards may include sharp bends, junctions, crossings, blind corners, steep gradients or roadworks.

170 Suitable road markings and signs should also be used to alert drivers to any restrictions which apply to the use of a traffic route. Adequate directions should also be provided to relevant parts of a work-place. Buildings, departments, entrances etc should be clearly marked, where necessary, so that unplanned manoeuvres are avoided.

171 Signs should comply with the Health and Safety (Safety Signs and Signals) Regulations 1996, although any signs used in connection with traffic should comply with the Traffic Signs Regulations and General Directions 2002 (as amended) (SI 2002 No 3113) and the Highway Code for use on public roads.

172 Where large vehicles have to reverse, consider measures for reducing risks to pedestrians and any people in wheelchairs, such as:
- *restricting reversing to places where it can be carried out safely;*
- *keeping people on foot or in wheelchairs away;*
- *providing suitable high-visibility clothing for people who are per-mitted in the area;*
- *fitting reversing alarms to warn the driver of an obstruction or apply the brakes automatically;*
- *employing banksmen to supervise the safe movement of vehicles; or*
- *built-in CCTV devices.*

173 Whatever measures are adopted, a safe system of work should operate at all times. Take account of people with impaired sight or hearing.

174 If crowds of people are likely to overflow on to roadways, for example at the end of a shift, consider stopping vehicles from using the routes at such times.

175 Building Regulations have requirements on protection from falling, collision and impact1,2 and further guidance is available from HSE's workplace transport safety website (www.hse.gov.uk/work-placetransport) and in related HSE publications.32,3

Conclusions

Post ERRA 2013, even though the Regulations may not give rise to a breach of statutory duty, the Workplace Regulations and in particular the APOC guidelines as to how they should be interpreted, are very useful evidence as to the likely common law duty of care involving not just slip, and trip claims, but a variety of other workplace accidents, as set out above.

CHAPTER SEVEN
ACCIDENTS AT HEIGHT:
THE 2005 WORK AT HEIGHT
REGULATIONS, LIABILITY
INVESTIGATIONS, KEY CASES
AND PROVING NEGLIGENCE

An important area in workplace accident litigation is accidents that occur at Heights, such as ladders, scaffolding or any other accident.

The 2005 Regulations

The 2005 Work at Height Regulations deal with legislation concerning accidents occurring at Height. Whilst again it is correct to say that the Regulations are not actionable as breaches of statutory duty for post October 2013 cases, they are a good guide to the likely standards of duty to be imposed upon employers, when considering negligence.

Application of the Regulations

The 2005 Regulations set out:-

Application
3.—(1) These Regulations shall apply—
(a) in Great Britain; and
(b) outside Great Britain as sections 1 to 59 and 80 to 82 of the 1974 Act apply by virtue of the Health and Safety at Work etc. Act 1974 (Application outside Great Britain) Order 2001(1).
(2) The requirements imposed by these Regulations on an employer shall apply in relation to work—
(a) by an employee of his; or
(b) by any other person under his control, to the extent of his control.
(3) The requirements imposed by these Regulations on an employer shall also apply to—
(a) a self-employed person, in relation to work—

(I) by him; or
(ii) by a person under his control, to the extent of his control; and
(b) to any person other than a self-employed person, in relation to work by a person under his control, to the extent of his control.

The Key Parts of the Regulations

The Key Sections of the 2005 Regulations are set out as follows:-

Organisation and planning

4.—(1) Every employer shall ensure that work at height is—
(a) properly planned;
(b) appropriately supervised; and
(c) carried out in a manner which is so far as is reasonably practicable safe,
and that its planning includes the selection of work equipment in accordance with regulation 7.
(2) Reference in paragraph (1) to planning of work includes planning for emergencies and rescue.
(3) Every employer shall ensure that work at height is carried out only when the weather conditions do not jeopardise the health or safety of persons involved in the work.
(4) Paragraph (3) shall not apply where members of the police, fire, ambulance or other emergency services are acting in an emergency

Thus, in a Work At Height Regulation case, one will likely seek disclosure of the Work at Height Risk Assessments, supervision records, method statements and plan for the Work

Competence
5. Every employer shall ensure that no person engages in any activity, including organisation, planning and supervision, in relation to work at height or work equipment for use in such work unless he is competent to do so or, if being trained, is being supervised by a competent person.

One will wish to see training records for the employee in relation to the Work at Height task, together with training records for the person supervising the task.

Avoidance of risks from work at height

6.—*(1) In identifying the measures required by this regulation, every employer shall take account of a risk assessment under regulation 3 of the Management Regulations.*

(2) Every employer shall ensure that work is not carried out at height where it is reasonably practicable to carry out the work safely otherwise than at height.

(3) Where work is carried out at height, every employer shall take suitable and sufficient measures to prevent, so far as is reasonably practicable, any person falling a distance liable to cause personal injury.

(4) The measures required by paragraph (3) shall include—

(a) his ensuring that the work is carried out—

(I) from an existing place of work; or

(ii) (in the case of obtaining access or egress) using an existing means, which complies with Schedule 1, where it is reasonably practicable to carry it out safely and under appropriate ergonomic conditions; and

(b) where it is not reasonably practicable for the work to be carried out in accordance with sub-paragraph (a), his providing sufficient work equipment for preventing, so far as is reasonably practicable, a fall occurring.

(5) Where the measures taken under paragraph (4) do not eliminate the risk of a fall occurring, every employer shall—

(a) so far as is reasonably practicable, provide sufficient work equipment to minimise—

(i) the distance and consequences; or

(ii) where it is not reasonably practicable to minimise the distance, the consequences, of a fall; and

(b) without prejudice to the generality of paragraph (3), provide such additional training and instruction or take other additional suitable and sufficient measures to prevent, so far as is reasonably practicable, any person falling a distance liable to cause personal injury.

This part of the Regulations is key. The Claimant will want to seek disclosure of how the risk assessments addressed the issue of how Working from Heights could be avoided. The Claimant should always be asked in conference if any other suitable method could have been adopted to avoid Working at Height. For example on a building site, could access have been gained from the existing building, as opposed to using a ladder?

> ### Selection of work equipment for work at height
> 7.—(1) Every employer, in selecting work equipment for use in work at height, shall—
> (a) give collective protection measures priority over personal protection measures; and
> (b) take account of—
> (I) the working conditions and the risks to the safety of persons at the place where the work equipment is to be used;
> (ii) in the case of work equipment for access and egress, the distance to be negotiated;
> (iii) the distance and consequences of a potential fall;
> (iv) the duration and frequency of use;
> (v) the need for easy and timely evacuation and rescue in an emergency;
> (vi) any additional risk posed by the use, installation or removal of that work equipment or by evacuation and rescue from it; and
> (vii) the other provisions of these Regulations.
> (2) An employer shall select work equipment for work at height which
> —
> (a) has characteristics including dimensions which—
> (I) are appropriate to the nature of the work to be performed and the foreseeable loadings; and
> (ii) allow passage without risk; and
> (b) is in other respects the most suitable work equipment, having regard in particular to the purposes specified in regulation 6.

The Defendant should always be asked to disclose the risk assessment regarding the selection of work equipment, if the accident was caused in whole or in part by the work equipment, and method statements concerning the selection of the equipment.

Inspection of places of work at height
13. Every employer shall so far as is reasonably practicable ensure that the surface and every parapet, permanent rail or other such fall protection measure of every place of work at height are checked on each occasion before the place is used.

So for example, if there has been a fall from scaffolding or a fall on scaffolding, records should be obtained to confirm the area was checked, prior to the employees being allowed into the work area.

Requirements for particular work equipment
8. Every employer shall ensure that, in the case of—
(a) a guard-rail, toe-board, barrier or similar collective means of protection, Schedule 2 is complied with;
(b) a working platform—
(I) Part 1 of Schedule 3 is complied with; and
(ii) where scaffolding is provided, Part 2 of Schedule 3 is also complied with;
(c) a net, airbag or other collective safeguard for arresting falls which is not part of a personal fall protection system, Schedule 4 is complied with;
(d) a personal fall protection system, Part 1 of Schedule 5 and—
(i) in the case of a work positioning system, Part 2 of Schedule 5;
(ii) in the case of rope access and positioning techniques, Part 3 of Schedule 5;
(iii) in the case of a fall arrest system, Part 4 of Schedule 5;
(iv) in the case of a work restraint system, Part 5 of Schedule 5,
are complied with; and
(e) a ladder, Schedule 6 is complied with.

Regulation 8 deals with fall safety systems, for various types of Work at Height equipment. Again where they are applicable, the risk assessments and method statements for the fall protection system should be requested. Further details are set out in the schedules as follows, for various methods of Work at Height equipment, and it is useful to set these out in full:-

SCHEDULE 1
REQUIREMENTS FOR EXISTING PLACES OF WORK AND MEANS OF ACCESS OR EGRESS AT HEIGHT

Every existing place of work or means of access or egress at height shall
—

(a) be stable and of sufficient strength and rigidity for the purpose for which it is intended to be or is being used;

(b) where applicable, rest on a stable, sufficiently strong surface;

(c) be of sufficient dimensions to permit the safe passage of persons and the safe use of any plant or materials required to be used and to provide a safe working area having regard to the work to be carried out there;

(d) possess suitable and sufficient means for preventing a fall;

(e) possess a surface which has no gap—

(i) through which a person could fall;

(ii) through which any material or object could fall and injure a person; or

(iii) giving rise to other risk of injury to any person, unless measures have been taken to protect persons against such risk;

(f) be so constructed and used, and maintained in such condition, as to prevent, so far as is reasonably practicable—

(I) the risk of slipping or tripping; or

(ii) any person being caught between it and any adjacent structure;

(g) where it has moving parts, be prevented by appropriate devices from moving inadvertently during work at height.

SCHEDULE 2
REQUIREMENTS FOR GUARD-RAILS, TOE-BOARDS, BARRIERS AND SIMILAR COLLECTIVE MEANS OF PROTECTION

1. Unless the context otherwise requires, any reference in this Schedule to means of protection is to a guard-rail, toe-board, barrier or similar collective means of protection.

2. Means of protection shall—

(a) be of sufficient dimensions, of sufficient strength and rigidity for the purposes for which they are being used, and otherwise suitable;

(b) be so placed, secured and used as to ensure, so far as is reasonably practicable, that they do not become accidentally displaced; and

(c) be so placed as to prevent, so far as is practicable, the fall of any person, or of any material or object, from any place of work.

3. In relation to work at height involved in construction work—

(a) the top guard-rail or other similar means of protection shall be at least 950 millimetres or, in the case of such means of protection already fixed at the coming into force of these Regulations, at least 910 millimetres above the edge from which any person is liable to fall;

(b) toe-boards shall be suitable and sufficient to prevent the fall of any person, or any material or object, from any place of work; and

(c) any intermediate guard-rail or similar means of protection shall be positioned so that any gap between it and other means of protection does not exceed 470 millimetres.

4. Any structure or part of a structure which supports means of protection or to which means of protection are attached shall be of sufficient strength and suitable for the purpose of such support or attachment.

5.—(1) Subject to sub-paragraph (2), there shall not be a lateral opening in means of protection save at a point of access to a ladder or stairway where an opening is necessary.

(2) Means of protection shall be removed only for the time and to the extent necessary to gain access or egress or for the performance of a particular task and shall be replaced as soon as practicable.

(3) The task shall not be performed while means of protection are removed unless effective compensatory safety measures are in place.

SCHEDULE 3
REQUIREMENTS FOR WORKING PLATFORMS

PART 1
REQUIREMENTS FOR ALL WORKING PLATFORMS
Interpretation
1. In this Schedule, "supporting structure" means any structure used for the purpose of supporting a working platform and includes any plant used for that purpose.
Condition of surfaces

2. Any surface upon which any supporting structure rests shall be stable, of sufficient strength and of suitable composition safely to support the supporting structure, the working platform and any loading intended to be placed on the working platform.

Stability of supporting structure

3. Any supporting structure shall—

(a) be suitable and of sufficient strength and rigidity for the purpose for which it is being used;

(b) in the case of a wheeled structure, be prevented by appropriate devices from moving inadvertently during work at height;

(c) in other cases, be prevented from slipping by secure attachment to the bearing surface or to another structure, provision of an effective anti-slip device or by other means of equivalent effectiveness;

(d) be stable while being erected, used and dismantled; and

(e) when altered or modified, be so altered or modified as to ensure that it remains stable.

Stability of working platforms

4. A working platform shall—

(a) be suitable and of sufficient strength and rigidity for the purpose or purposes for which it is intended to be used or is being used;

(b) be so erected and used as to ensure that its components do not become accidentally displaced so as to endanger any person;

(c) when altered or modified, be so altered or modified as to ensure that it remains stable; and

(d) be dismantled in such a way as to prevent accidental displacement.

Safety on working platforms

5. A working platform shall—

(a) be of sufficient dimensions to permit the safe passage of persons and the safe use of any plant or materials required to be used and to provide a safe working area having regard to the work being carried out there;

(b) possess a suitable surface and, in particular, be so constructed that the surface of the working platform has no gap—

(i) through which a person could fall;

(ii) through which any material or object could fall and injure a person; or

(iii) giving rise to other risk of injury to any person, unless measures have been taken to protect persons against such risk; and

(c) be so erected and used, and maintained in such condition, as to prevent, so far as is reasonably practicable—

(i) the risk of slipping or tripping; or

(ii) any person being caught between the working platform and any adjacent structure.

Loading

6. *A working platform and any supporting structure shall not be loaded so as to give rise to a risk of collapse or to any deformation which could affect its safe use.*

PART 2

ADDITIONAL REQUIREMENTS FOR SCAFFOLDING

Additional requirements for scaffolding

7. *Strength and stability calculations for scaffolding shall be carried out unless—*

(a) a note of the calculations, covering the structural arrangements contemplated, is available; or

(b) it is assembled in conformity with a generally recognised standard configuration.

8. *Depending on the complexity of the scaffolding selected, an assembly, use and dismantling plan shall be drawn up by a competent person. This may be in the form of a standard plan, supplemented by items relating to specific details of the scaffolding in question.*

9. *A copy of the plan, including any instructions it may contain, shall be kept available for the use of persons concerned in the assembly, use, dismantling or alteration of scaffolding until it has been dismantled.*

10. *The dimensions, form and layout of scaffolding decks shall be appropriate to the nature of the work to be performed and suitable for the loads to be carried and permit work and passage in safety.*

11. *While a scaffold is not available for use, including during its assembly, dismantling or alteration, it shall be marked with general warning signs in accordance with the Health and Safety (Safety Signs and Signals) Regulations 1996(1) and be suitably delineated by physical means preventing access to the danger zone.*

12. *Scaffolding may be assembled, dismantled or significantly altered only under the supervision of a competent person and by persons who have received appropriate and specific training in the operations*

envisaged which addresses specific risks which the operations may entail and precautions to be taken, and more particularly in—
(a) understanding of the plan for the assembly, dismantling or alteration of the scaffolding concerned;
(b) safety during the assembly, dismantling or alteration of the scaffolding concerned;
(c) measures to prevent the risk of persons, materials or objects falling;
(d) safety measures in the event of changing weather conditions which could adversely affect the safety of the scaffolding concerned;
(e) permissible loadings;
(f) any other risks which the assembly, dismantling or alteration of the scaffolding may entail.

SCHEDULE 4
REQUIREMENTS FOR COLLECTIVE SAFEGUARDS FOR ARRESTING FALLS
1. Any reference in this Schedule to a safeguard is to a collective safeguard for arresting falls.
2. A safeguard shall be used only if—
(a) a risk assessment has demonstrated that the work activity can so far as is reasonably practicable be performed safely while using it and without affecting its effectiveness;
(b) the use of other, safer work equipment is not reasonably practicable; and
(c) a sufficient number of available persons have received adequate training specific to the safeguard, including rescue procedures.
3. A safeguard shall be suitable and of sufficient strength to arrest safely the fall of any person who is liable to fall.
4. A safeguard shall—
(a) in the case of a safeguard which is designed to be attached, be securely attached to all the required anchors, and the anchors and the means of attachment thereto shall be suitable and of sufficient strength and stability for the purpose of safely supporting the foreseeable loading in arresting any fall and during any subsequent rescue;
(b) in the case of an airbag, landing mat or similar safeguard, be stable; and

(c) in the case of a safeguard which distorts in arresting a fall, afford sufficient clearance.

5. *Suitable and sufficient steps shall be taken to ensure, so far as practicable, that in the event of a fall by any person the safeguard does not itself cause injury to that person.*

SCHEDULE 5
REQUIREMENTS FOR PERSONAL FALL PROTECTION SYSTEMS

PART 1
REQUIREMENTS FOR ALL PERSONAL FALL PROTECTION SYSTEMS

1. *A personal fall protection system shall be used only if—*
(a) a risk assessment has demonstrated that—
(I) the work can so far as is reasonably practicable be performed safely while using that system; and
(ii) the use of other, safer work equipment is not reasonably practicable; and
(b) the user and a sufficient number of available persons have received adequate training specific to the operations envisaged, including rescue procedures.
2. *A personal fall protection system shall—*
(a) be suitable and of sufficient strength for the purposes for which it is being used having regard to the work being carried out and any foreseeable loading;
(b) where necessary, fit the user;
(c) be correctly fitted;
(d) be designed to minimise injury to the user and, where necessary, be adjusted to prevent the user falling or slipping from it, should a fall occur; and
(e) be so designed, installed and used as to prevent unplanned or uncontrolled movement of the user.
3. *A personal fall protection system designed for use with an anchor shall be securely attached to at least one anchor, and each anchor and the means of attachment thereto shall be suitable and of sufficient*

strength and stability for the purpose of supporting any foreseeable loading.

4. Suitable and sufficient steps shall be taken to prevent any person falling or slipping from a personal fall protection system.

PART 2
ADDITIONAL REQUIREMENTS FOR WORK POSITIONING SYSTEMS

A work positioning system shall be used only if either—

(a) the system includes a suitable backup system for preventing or arresting a fall; and

(b) where the system includes a line as a backup system, the user is connected to it; or

(c) where it is not reasonably practicable to comply with sub-paragraph (a), all practicable measures are taken to ensure that the work positioning system does not fail.

PART 3
ADDITIONAL REQUIREMENTS FOR ROPE ACCESS AND POSITIONING TECHNIQUES

1. A rope access or positioning technique shall be used only if—

(a) subject to paragraph 3, it involves a system comprising at least two separately anchored lines, of which one ("the working line") is used as a means of access, egress and support and the other is the safety line;

(b) the user is provided with a suitable harness and is connected by it to the working line and the safety line;

(c) the working line is equipped with safe means of ascent and descent and has a self-locking system to prevent the user falling should he lose control of his movements; and

(d) the safety line is equipped with a mobile fall protection system which is connected to and travels with the user of the system.

2. Taking the risk assessment into account and depending in particular on the duration of the job and the ergonomic constraints, provision must be made for a seat with appropriate accessories.

3. The system may comprise a single rope where—

(a) a risk assessment has demonstrated that the use of a second line would entail higher risk to persons; and

(b) appropriate measures have been taken to ensure safety.

PART 4
ADDITIONAL REQUIREMENTS FOR FALL ARREST SYSTEMS
1. A fall arrest system shall incorporate a suitable means of absorbing energy and limiting the forces applied to the user's body.
2. A fall arrest system shall not be used in a manner—
(a) which involves the risk of a line being cut;
(b) where its safe use requires a clear zone (allowing for any pendulum effect), which does not afford such zone; or
(c) which otherwise inhibits its performance or renders its use unsafe.

PART 5
ADDITIONAL REQUIREMENTS FOR WORK RESTRAINT SYSTEMS
A work restraint system shall—
(a) be so designed that, if used correctly, it prevents the user from getting into a position in which a fall can occur; and
(b) be used correctly.

Ladders

Many accidents at work involve ladders, and there are particular requirements in Schedule 6 as follows:-

SCHEDULE 6
REQUIREMENTS FOR LADDERS
1. Every employer shall ensure that a ladder is used for work at height only if a risk assessment under regulation 3 of the Management Regulations has demonstrated that the use of more suitable work equipment is not justified because of the low risk and—
(a) the short duration of use; or
(b) existing features on site which he cannot alter.
2. Any surface upon which a ladder rests shall be stable, firm, of sufficient strength and of suitable composition safely to support the ladder so that its rungs or steps remain horizontal, and any loading intended to be placed on it.

3. A ladder shall be so positioned as to ensure its stability during use.

4. A suspended ladder shall be attached in a secure manner and so that, with the exception of a flexible ladder, it cannot be displaced and swinging is prevented.

5. A portable ladder shall be prevented from slipping during use by—

(a) securing the stiles at or near their upper or lower ends;

(b) an effective anti-slip or other effective stability device; or

(c) any other arrangement of equivalent effectiveness.

6. A ladder used for access shall be long enough to protrude sufficiently above the place of landing to which it provides access, unless other measures have been taken to ensure a firm handhold.

7. No interlocking or extension ladder shall be used unless its sections are prevented from moving relative to each other while in use.

8. A mobile ladder shall be prevented from moving before it is stepped on.

9. Where a ladder or run of ladders rises a vertical distance of 9 metres or more above its base, there shall, where reasonably practicable, be provided at suitable intervals sufficient safe landing areas or rest platforms.

10. Every ladder shall be used in such a way that—

(a) a secure handhold and secure support are always available to the user; and

(b) the user can maintain a safe handhold when carrying a load unless, in the case of a step ladder, the maintenance of a handhold is not practicable when a load is carried, and a risk assessment under regulation 3 of the Management Regulations has demonstrated that the use of a step-pladder is justified because of—

(I) the low risk; and

(ii) the short duration of use.

Construction Site Accidents and Working at Height

There is a separate chapter in this book concerning construction site accidents, but in the context of the Work at Height Regulations, Regulation 10 is helpful in relation to falling objects, for example from scaffolding:-

Falling objects

10.—(1) Every employer shall, where necessary to prevent injury to any person, take suitable and sufficient steps to prevent, so far as is reasonably practicable, the fall of any material or object.

(2) Where it is not reasonably practicable to comply with the requirements of paragraph (1), every employer shall take suitable and sufficient steps to prevent any person being struck by any falling material or object which is liable to cause personal injury.

(3) Every employer shall ensure that no material or object is thrown or tipped from height in circumstances where it is liable to cause injury to any person.

(4) Every employer shall ensure that materials and objects are stored in such a way as to prevent risk to any person arising from the collapse, overturning or unintended movement of such materials or objects.

Regulation 11, also sets out that, where there is a risk of falling objects there should be an area preventing unauthorised people from entering. This is again likely to be relevant to construction sites, for example where demolition work is being undertaken.

Danger areas

11. Without prejudice to the preceding requirements of these Regulations, every employer shall ensure that—

(a) where a workplace contains an area in which, owing to the nature of the work, there is a risk of any person at work—

(i) falling a distance; or

(ii) being struck by a falling object,

which is liable to cause personal injury, the workplace is so far as is reasonably practicable equipped with devices preventing unauthorised persons from entering such area; and

(b) such area is clearly indicated.

Work at Height – A Case in Point

Jason Sharp v Top Flight Scaffolding Limited [2013 EWHC 478 QB] is a good example of a Work at Height case and the facts were as follows:-

4. *The claimant, whose date of birth is 13 May 1969 and who is therefore 43 years old, had worked as a scaffolder for many years, and indeed for a number of years he had worked for the defendant, and in fact, it is common ground that he had known Mr Bolton, the sole director of the defendant, for very many years and had worked for another company owned by Mr Bolton before being employed by the defendant.*

5. *On 23 November 2009, the claimant and his nephew, Ray Eastmond, who, it is common ground, was employed, albeit on a self-employed basis, from time to time as an unqualified scaffolder's labourer, attended at the defendant's yard and, as was usual, were given a list of jobs for the day (3/14/238(a)). It was Mr Eastmond's evidence that the claimant was in charge and Mr Eastmond did what he was told by the claimant in all matters.*

6. *The list of jobs for that day involved a pick-up of equipment from an address in Purley, the dismantling of scaffolding at an address in Sanderstead, and the erection of a scaffold at the rear of the Property, which was a terraced property, which meant that the claimant and Mr Eastmond would have to transport the scaffolding equipment through the house and into the back garden.*

7. *It was intended that the scaffold was to be used by a regular customer of the defendant, a roofing company called Ray Jones Roofing.*

8. *The bundle of photographs at 1/15H/135 and following includes a number of photographs taken of the lorry which was used by the claimant and Mr Eastmond on the day of the accident, from which, it is common ground, it is plain that on the day of the accident, whether because they had been specifically loaded on the lorry at the defendant's yard by Mr Eastmond and the claimant under the claimant's supervision, or picked up by the claimant and Mr Eastmond from the other two jobs to which they had been directed that day, the claimant had available for his use in connection with the proposed scaffolding a number (four) of ladders of varying*

lengths. There was one ladder 7.07 metres in length, and three shorter ladders of 4.09 metres, 2.95 metres and 2.91 metres respectively, as measured by Peter Collingwood of the Health and Safety Executive during the course of his investigation into the accident, as can be seen from his investigation report with recommendations, a copy of which is at 1/15/84 at page 88.

9. *It is common ground that no-one from the defendant had attended at the Property in advance, Mr Bolton's evidence being that the job had been phoned or faxed through late the previous week with him having been provided with a very basic design, a copy of which is at 3/12/237. He had also spoken to the householder about access, and been told that access could be effected through the house, a not unusual situation with such terraced houses.*

10. *It is common ground that, because of the configuration of the downstairs of the Property, at least some of the scaffolding equipment, and specifically long poles, had to be brought through the Property via the small toilet window which can be seen at the rear of the single-storey building shown in the photographs at, for example, pages 129 and 130. These also demonstrate the very basic nature of the scaffold structure as erected by the claimant.*

11. *It also appears to be common ground that, for some reason, and this is certainly the uncontroverted evidence of Mr Eastmond, no attempt was made to take any ladders through the house at this stage, and specifically not the long ladder, which it appears the claimant intended to use as the means of access and egress from the scaffold he was intending to erect.*

12. *It is common ground that, once the equipment necessary to erect the scaffolding, such as boards and pipework, but not any ladders, had been taken through the Property to the rear, the scaffold was constructed by the claimant with Mr Eastmond handing him the equipment as necessary, and that there came a time when the only item to be completed was the fixing of an external ladder access. At this point the claimant was at the top of the scaffolding structure*

with no safe means of descending whilst Mr Eastmond was, of course, at ground level and Mr Eastmond's evidence was to the effect that, whilst the claimant had been in the course of erecting the scaffolding structure, he (Mr Eastmond) had tried but failed to lift the long ladder through the toilet window, and indeed, it appears to be common ground that the long ladder could not be taken through the Property as appears from paragraph 5.4 of the Defence (1/4/11 at 13).

13. *At this point, the claimant sent Mr Eastmond back to the lorry, which was parked nearby, to telephone Mr Bolton. There is some dispute as to the precise purposes of this telephone call, and slightly different accounts have been given by Mr Eastmond at different times, but to my mind nothing turns on this issue. What is certain is that, whilst Mr Eastmond was making the telephone call to Mr Bolton, the claimant fell from the scaffolding, landing in the neighbouring property. No-one saw him fall.*

14. *There are only two possible explanations for the fall: either the claimant fell through the gap where the external ladder was to be fitted, or he fell whilst attempting to climb down the outside of the scaffolding. Given that he fell into the neighbouring property, the only sensible conclusion is that the latter is the more likely explanation, and I so conclude.*

In relation to primary liability, the Judge made reference to some further guidance which one may consider if conducting a Work at Height case:-

17. *In 1995, the Health and Safety Executive published a booklet entitled "Health and Safety for Small Construction Sites". This advocated the use of a single external ladder to the working lift of scaffolding (2/1/3).*

18. *On 29 December 1999, the Management of Health and Safety at Work Regulations 1999 came into force, providing, among other things, a requirement that every employer should make a*

suitable and sufficient assessment of the risks of health and safety of his employees to which they are exposed whilst at work.

19. *In 2000, the **National Access and Scaffolding Federation (NASC) produced Guidance Note SG4:00**, which included the following:*
"Ladder access
1 In fact, there is no issue as to whether or not the wearing of personal fall protection would have made a difference on the facts of this case.

(1) Ladders for use by scaffolders should be included as early as possible into the erection process and removed as late as possible during dismantling, reducing the need for scaffolders to climb the scaffold structure.

(2) It is recommended that a ladder bay is constructed and that ladders are incorporated from top to bottom of the scaffolding structure." (2/2/6).

20. *In January 2005 and in anticipation of the Work at Height Regulations 2005 coming into force, the **NASC produced further technical guidance TG20:05, entitled "Guide to Good Practice: Scaffolding with Tubes and Fittings"**, which provided as follows (2/8/25):-*

"16. Access to and in scaffolds.

16.1 General
The Work at Height Regulations require employers to use existing structures for access to work at height, where reasonably practicable. For example, if a permanent staircase or passenger lift could be utilised to access and egress a tall building at high level, thus avoiding the need to expose scaffolders to an unnecessary risk of a fall whilst erecting, altering and dismantling a temporary scaffolding access tower, then the permanent access should be used.

Access and egress to and from scaffolding should be considered using the following hierarchy of access:

1. *Staircases.*
2. *Ladder access bays with single lift ladders.*
3. *Ladder access bays with multiple lift ladders.*
4. *Internal ladder access with a protected ladder trap.*
5. *External ladder access using a safety gate.*

Work at Height Regulations require Risk Assessments to show that ladders can be used if more suitable access equipment is not justified because of the low risk and short duration of use.

20. *The* **Work at Height Regulations 2005** *came into force on 6 April 2005. These included the following:*

4(1) Every employer shall ensure that work is— (a) properly planned;
(b) appropriately supervised; and
(c) carried out in a manner which is so far as is reasonably practicable safe, and that its planning includes the selection of work equipment in accordance with regulation 7.
5 Every employer shall ensure that no person engages in any activity, including organisation, planning and supervision, in relation to work at height or work equipment for use in such work unless he is competent to do so or, if being trained, is being supervised by a competent person.
6 (3) Where work is carried out at height, every employer shall take suitable and sufficient measures to prevent, so far as is reasonably practicable, any person falling a distance liable to cause personal injury.

22. *In July 2005,* **NASC published its Guidance Note SG4:05,** *which included the following:*

"6. Before scaffolders undertake work at height, it is essential to consider the work to be performed, and take account of any foreseeable hazards arising from that work that will need to be dealt with. To ensure the safety of scaffolders and others that may be affected by scaffolding and such operations, it is necessary for a suitably competent person to carry out a Risk Assessment.

15. *When carrying out a Risk Assessment, it is recommended that, where possible, an inspection of the site is undertaken by a suitably competent person. The purpose of the Assessment is to take due account of all foreseeable hazards in the workplace, in addition to any commercial considerations for the job." (2/5/12-13).*

23. *In March 2006, the* **NASC Guidance Note SG4:05 was updated** *and provided as follows:*
    "Safe access for use by scaffolders (e.g. staircase or ladder) should be incorporated as early as possible in the erection process (and removed as late as possible during dismantling), avoiding the need for scaffolders to climb the scaffold structure." (2/3/8).

24. *In November 2008,* **NASC Technical Guidance Note TG20:08 was published, updating TG20:05, but without altering the relevant text** *(2/4/10).*

25. *In 2009, the defendant produced its latest edition of its Health and Safety and Code of Conduct Booklet, which provided that site managers should:*
    "Ensure that all employees under their control receive sufficient and adequate training to enable them to undertake competently the work for which they are employed." (3/6/182).
    Evidence
    "Ensure that a written Risk Assessment is carried out in each site in which he has responsibility." (3/6/183)
    "The Director is responsible for Safety and the Health and Safety Consultants are responsible for recommending and arranging safety training and refresher courses for all employees as necessary." (3/6/192)

> *"...Scaffolding may only be used if erected by an approved contractor and inspected in accordance with best practices...the provisions of the Work at Height Regulations 2005 must be adhered to." (3/6/193)*
> *"Never climb up or down the outside of a scaffold, use the access ladders provided." (3/6/196)*

The parties positions were summed up in the Judgment as follows:-

32. *In essence, it is the claimant's case (paragraph 10 of the Particulars of Claim) (1/2/4) that, had a proper risk assessment been carried out and the guidance provided by NASC been heeded, in particular SG4:00, TG20:08 and SG4:05, a Method Statement should have been provided to the claimant providing for the incorporation of internal ladder access, which should have taken precedence over external ladder access so as to avoid the need for one long ladder externally from ground to the working platform at eaves height, such that the accident would not have happened. In this regard, a number of allegations of negligence and breach of various statutory duties are alleged. In the alternative, it is said on behalf of the claimant that any finding of contributory negligence should be very low, particularly in the light of the alleged failings on the part of the defendant.*

33. *The defendant, by contrast, relies on the fact that the claimant was an experienced scaffolder who, it was said, was perfectly capable both of assessing the work for himself and of erecting a safe scaffold, for which he had sufficient training and for which he had the necessary equipment available to him to undertake its construction safely with internal ladder access and egress, there being no time pressure. Reliance is also placed on a generic Risk Assessment (3/15/239) and on the toolbox training said to have been given by the external provider. It is also said that the decision to climb down the scaffold was the claimant's and the claimant's alone, and that he knew that to climb down was dangerous; in short, what is alleged is that the overriding cause of the accident was the fact that the claimant had failed to use short ladders in breach of his*

training and instructions, and that when the problem manifested itself, by climbing over the side. It must have been obvious to the claimant that there would have been a problem bringing the long ladder through the Property, and he must have known that he had short ladders available on the lorry because he would have been involved in the loading of them, either at the defendant's yard or when the scaffold at Sanderstead was dismantled earlier in the day. In the alternative, the defendant asserts that the accident was caused in substantial part by the claimant's own negligence.

The Judge made the following decision:-

34. *It is common ground that the approach in law to breach of duty is as set out in Bhatt v Fontaine Motors [2010] EWCA Civ 863, where Richards LJ, with whom Sedley and Sullivan LJJ agreed, set out the position at [28] at follows:*

   "I agree that one needs to start with the Regulations rather than with the claimant's conduct. The Regulations are directed at avoiding or minimising the risks inherent in working at height. The point is well made in the simple hierarchy set out in the Health and Safety Executive's guide (see [15] above), that is, work at height must be avoided altogether if is reasonably practicable to carry out the work otherwise than at height: that is the focus of Regulation 6(2). If work at height cannot be avoided, the risk must be minimised by, inter alia, the selection of work equipment which is appropriate and meets the other requirements in Regulation 7(2)..."

35. *It follows that, in respect of primary liability, the claimant has to establish a causative breach of duty. In my judgment, on the facts of this case, this is established on the balance of probabilities beyond peradventure. At best, the claimant had had no formal training since the 1990s, assuming that he did in fact pass the Part 2 scaffolding basic test (of which there is no documentary evidence), and at worst he had had no training, as opposed to undergoing an assessment in 1998, when what was acceptable was very different,*

as is apparent from a perusal of the changing guidance issued, to which I have referred earlier in this judgment, since when, at best, he has had a couple of toolbox talks in 2006 and 2008 in respect of the content of which again there is no documentary evidence. Whilst the claimant may have been competent in 1998, when he successfully passed the assessment, best practice has moved on substantially since then and, in my judgment, the training facilities provided by the defendant can best be characterised as lamentable and the defendant has plainly failed in its common law duty to provide the claimant with adequate training and has failed in its duty to ensure that the claimant remained competent to engage in the organisation, planning and erection of scaffolding.

36. *The lack of training and the level of ignorance on the part of Mr Bolton of the defendant and its employee, Mr Hardy is, in my judgment, aptly demonstrated in their respective witness statements, since nowhere in either statement does either Mr Bolton or Mr Hardy criticise the claimant for not having utilised internal access ladders. Still worse, they do not criticise him for apparently intending to use an external ladder notwithstanding the clear hierarchy set out in the January 2005 guidance (NASC Technical Guidance TG20:05), nor the decision to proceed with the construction of the scaffold without any safe means of access or egress; no attempt having been made even to try and bring the long ladder through the Property. It is difficult to imagine clearer examples of the level of ignorance of both Mr Hardy and Mr Bolton and, of course, in this regard it is also pertinent to recall the evidence of Mr Bolton that he regarded the claimant as being better trained than he himself was, he not having attended any relevant courses himself"*

37. *In all the circumstances, given that that was the evidence of the prevailing attitude of the sole director, being the director responsible for safety, and a fellow scaffolding worker, it is perhaps not surprising that the claimant should have constructed the scaffold at the Property without any internal ladders, and indeed without any ready and safe means of access or egress. There was, to my mind,*

also a systematic disregard by the defendant of its own health and safety policy, since it plainly failed to ensure that all employees under its control received sufficient and adequate training to enable them to undertake competently the work for which they were employed, and since it plainly failed to ensure that a written risk assessment was carried out on each site. Reliance on the claimant's suggested ability to assess the job for himself without the need of a risk assessment or method statement, given as I find his lack of relevant training, simply will not do.

38. *In this regard, it is perhaps noteworthy that in his report, Mr Warnes, as I have already recorded, identified management failings and a lack of pre-planning as reasons for the accident. When confronted by these findings of such failings, Mr Bolton initially sought to deny them and only reluctantly, when pressed, did he accept that there were failings, although even then he sought to characterise them as "small" failings. In this regard, it is important to recall that the whole purpose of the Regulations is to protect employees against the dangers inherent in working at height. They are to guard against carelessness and lapses in concentration, and in that context Mr Bolton's characterisation of failings as being "small" failings is perhaps a further indication of his generally lax approach to issues of safety.*

39. **Had the claimant been properly trained and, had there been a site-specific Risk Assessment undertaken, and an up-to-date Method Statement supplied, the claimant would, in all probability, have incorporated the use of internal ladders, which he plainly knew he had available to him, in the construction of the scaffold, and this tragic accident could have been avoided. In my judgment, primary liability is plainly made out. On the facts of this case the defendant simply cannot rely on the claimant's on site assessment".**

However the Judgment also highlights useful findings in relation to contributory negligence and the test to be applied:-

41. *I have been referred to a number of authorities by counsel in their very helpful closing submissions, the most relevant of which is* **Sherlock v Chester City Council [2004] EWCA Civ 201.** *In that case, the claimant operated a portable bench saw and the defendant did not provide a risk assessment or training since it considered that the claimant had sufficient experience. Problems were caused by the length of facias which were to be cut, and which had a habit of bowing, but no run-off bench was provided to prevent bowing. The defendant admitted breach of Regulation 20 of the Provision and Use of Work Equipment Regulations 1998.*

42. *On the issue of primary liability, Latham LJ, with whom Auld and Arden LJJ agreed, concluded as follows:*

> *"30. I entirely accept that this is not a case of mere inattention, which was the mischief referred to by Lord Tucker. But requirements of both common law and the regulations which I have identified have, as part of their purpose, the objective of ensuring that both employer and employee have taken stock of the situation where an appropriate work practice has to be identified so as to ensure that each has in mind the relevant risk and the necessary measures to obviate or reduce it. For the reasons that I have given, that was an obligation on the respondents, going beyond the actions and the decisions of the appellant, and which was causative of the accident. It cannot therefore be said here that the fault of the appellant was co- extensive with the fault of the respondent. The respondent's negligence and breaches of statutory duty were, accordingly, a cause of the accident."*

43. *Having so concluded, Latham LJ then turned to the question of contributory negligence in the following passage:*

> *"31. The question then arises as to the apportionment of liability. In Toole v Bolton Metropolitan Borough Council [2002] EWCA Civ 588, Buxton LJ said:*

'It is not usual for there to be marked findings of contributory negligence in a breach of statutory duty case'.

32. There may well be some justification for that view in cases of momentary inattention by an employee. But where a risk has been consciously accepted by an employee, it seems to me that different considerations may arise. That is particularly where the employee is skilled and the precaution in question is neither esoteric nor one which he could not take himself. In the present case, he could have made himself a run-off bench, or ensured that Mr Webb was there when he cut the relevant facia board. In those circumstances, it seems to me that the appellant can properly be required to bear the greater responsibility. I would assess his responsibility for the accident at 60%. Accordingly, he is entitled to 40% of whatever damages are ultimately considered to be appropriate for the dreadful injury he suffered to his hand."

In the index case the Judge concluded on this issue:-

44. *"For my part, I do not find the absence of any criticism of the claimant by Mr Warnes in his report as being in any way significant. Whatever may or may not be said in the report, the fact of the matter is, in my judgment, that the decision to climb down the outside of the scaffold was taken deliberately and in the knowledge that it was dangerous. Equally, the decision to construct scaffolding without any ready means of access/egress was a deliberate decision on the part of the claimant, which he must have realised exposed him to a risk of danger if in fact, as turned out to be the case, he had to climb down without the benefit of any ladders. These are matters of legitimate and serious criticism of the claimant's conduct. Whatever the failings of the defendant in terms of negligence and breach of statutory duty, in this case, to adopt the words of Latham LJ in Sherlock , the claimant consciously accepted the risk and the precaution was neither esoteric nor one which he could not take himself. In the circumstances, it seems to me that the claimant can*

properly be required to bear the greater responsibility, and I would assess his responsibility for the accident in this case at 60%.

Further Guidance

The Work at Height Regulations should be the first port of call, but in relation to specific examples, further guidance as to specific scenarios may be found in the following publications:-

Health and safety in roof work HSG33 (Fourth edition) HSE Books 2012 ISBN 978 0 7176 6527 3
www.hse.gov.uk/pubns/books/hsg33.htm

BS EN 365:2004 *Personal protective equipment against falls from a height: General requirements for instructions for use, maintenance, periodic examination, repair, marking and packaging* British Standards Institution

BS 5395-3:1985 *Stairs, ladders and walkways. Code of practice for the design of industrial type stairs, permanent ladders and walkways* British Standards Institution

BS 4211:2005+A1:2008 *Specification for permanently fixed ladders* British Standards Institution

Conclusions

Even in post October 2013 cases, the *Work at Height Regulations* are likely to still be important guidance as to the likely standard of care required by employees in cases where workers either fall from height or are struck by objects from height. In such cases the Regulations need to be considered carefully and pleadings together with the relevant codes of practice. Contributory negligence in Work at Height accidents always needs to be considered as per the case of *Sharp* and in particular whether the *"claimant consciously accepted the risk and the precaution was neither esoteric nor one which he could not take himself"*.

CHAPTER EIGHT
MANUAL HANDLING ACCIDENTS:
THE MANUAL HANDLING
OPERATIONS REGULATIONS 1992,
KEY CASES
AND PROVING NEGLIGENCE

The 1992 Regulations

The Regulations set out as follows:-

Duties of employers
4.—(1) Each employer shall—
(a) so far as is reasonably practicable, avoid the need for his employees to undertake any manual handling operations at work which involve a risk of their being injured; or
(b) where it is not reasonably practicable to avoid the need for his employees to undertake any manual handling operations at work which involve a risk of their being injured—
(i) make a suitable and sufficient assessment of all such manual handling operations to be undertaken by them, having regard to the factors which are specified in column 1 of Schedule 1 to these Regulations and considering the questions which are specified in the corresponding entry in column 2 of that Schedule,
(ii) take appropriate steps to reduce the risk of injury to those employees arising out of their undertaking any such manual handling operations to the lowest level reasonably practicable, and
(iii) take appropriate steps to provide any of those employees who are undertaking any such manual handling operations with general indications and, where it is reasonably practicable to do so, precise information on—
(aa) the weight of each load, and
(bb) the heaviest side of any load whose centre of gravity is not positioned centrally.

(2) Any assessment such as is referred to in paragraph (1)(b)(i) of this regulation shall be reviewed by the employer who made it if—
(a) there is reason to suspect that it is no longer valid; or
(b) there has been a significant change in the manual handling operations to which it relates; and where as a result of any such review changes to an assessment are required, the relevant employer shall make them.

Duty of employees

5. Each employee while at work shall make full and proper use of any system of work provided for his use by his employer in compliance with regulation 4(1)(b)(ii) of these Regulations.

SCHEDULE 1
FACTORS TO WHICH THE EMPLOYER MUST HAVE REGARD AND QUESTIONS HE MUST CONSIDER WHEN MAKING AN ASSESSMENT OF MANUAL HANDLING OPERATIONS

Column 1	Column 2
Factors	Questions

1. The tasks	**Do they involve:**
	    holding or manipulating loads at distance from trunk?
	    unsatisfactory bodily movement or posture, especially:
	        twisting the trunk?
	        stooping?
	        reaching upwards?
	    excessive movement of loads, especially:
	        excessive lifting or lowering distances?
	        excessive carrying distances?
	    excessive pushing or pulling of loads?
	    risk of sudden movement of loads?
	    frequent or prolonged physical effort?
	    insufficient rest or recovery periods?
	    a rate of work imposed by a process?

2. The loads	**Are they:** *heavy?*

	bulky or unwieldy?
	difficult to grasp?
	unstable, or with contents likely to shift?
	sharp, hot or otherwise potentially damaging?
3. The working environment	*Are there:*
	space constraints preventing good posture?
	uneven, slippery or unstable floors?
	variations in level of floors or work surfaces?
	extremes of temperature or humidity?
	conditions causing ventilation problems or gusts of wind?
	poor lighting conditions?
4. Individual capability	***Does the job:***
	require unusual strength, height, etc?
	create a hazard to those who might reasonably be considered to be pregnant or to have a health problem?
	require special information or training for its safe performance?
5. Other factors	***Is movement or posture hindered by personal protective equipment or by clothing?***

The Health and Safety (Miscellaneous Amendments) Regulations 2002 provide:

"Amendment of the Manual Handling Operations Regulations 1992
4. Regulation 4 of the Manual Handling Operations Regulations 1992 shall be amended by adding the following paragraph—
"(3) In determining for the purposes of this regulation whether manual handling operations at work involve a risk of injury and in determining the appropriate steps to reduce that risk regard shall be had in particular to—
(a) the physical suitability of the employee to carry out the operations;
(b) the clothing, footwear or other personal effects he is wearing;
(c) his knowledge and training;
(d) the results of any relevant risk assessment carried out pursuant to regulation 3 of the Management of Health and Safety at Work Regulations 1999;

(e) whether the employee is within a group of employees identified by that assessment as being especially at risk; and
(f) the results of any health surveillance provided pursuant to regulation 6 of the Management of Health and Safety Regulations 1999."

A Case in Point – Manual Handling

The following are examples of cases that failed under the HM Regulations. In **SHAUN NAREY v ICELAND FOODS LTD (2015)** the facts were as follows from the Judgment:-

> *"2. On 23 July 2011 the claimant, whilst carrying a plastic crate of shopping, including tins of dog food, for home delivery, lost his grip on the crate resulting in it falling on his right big toe with resulting injuries including a crush injury to the distal phalanx of his right big toe, a compound fracture.*
>
> *3. The claimant says that the defendant failed to provide personal protective equipment to him in the form of steel toe capped boots and was therefore in breach of the Manual Handling Regulations and Personal Protective Equipment at Work Regulations. The defendant admits injury occurred as a result of the accident and that it did not provide the claimant with protective footwear"*

The Law

> *"The burden of proving that the defendant has complied with the relevant regulations falls on the defendant. The defendant relies on the regulations set out above. The standard of proof is the civil standard on a balance of probabilities".*

[It should however be noted that post ERRA this would not longer be the case].

The Defendant argued that:-

"28. The defendant submits it fulfilled its duty under regulation 4(1) (b)(i) because it was not reasonably practicable to avoid the need for the claimant to carry out the manual handling operation and a risk assessment of the operation had been carried out.

29. In relation to regulation 4(l)(b)(ii) the defendant said it fulfilled its duty because it had reduced the risk to the lowest level reasonably practicable with the provision of suitable and safe equipment, training and instruction"

The Court found:-

*36. **I am satisfied that the risk assessment carried out was a "suitable and sufficient assessment of the identified risk to employees in handling the home delivery crates**. A maximum weight was imposed. Whilst the employees may not have had specific training on assessing weight I take into account that the loads were bags of shopping which could be seen as to content and about which any person could form a view as to weight and they had examples of weight every day. I do not consider that additional training on assessing weight would assist. Each load will be quite different. It would not be practical to weigh each load as that in itself would necessitate further lifting and handling. There is also another check in that the crates could not be overloaded as they would not then stack and this was part of training.*

*37. The crates may have been unstable the claimant suggests when one is balanced on another and it is moved with the weight supported. The claimant was shown how to do this. I accept the evidence of Mr Stevens that it is unlikely the contents would move to the extent that the there was a risk the crate would be dropped. **In any event such a risk had been assessed and training provided**. There were 2 sturdy grips on each crate, one for each hand to stabilise the crate during such an operation.*

*38. Whilst access to top crates may be assessed as a high risk, there is a policy that the stacks are not more than 5 crates high and only 4 if being moved. An **employee has a duty to keep himself safe and a*** *shorter person could have problem, in which case he or she must seek help. That is part of the training.*

39. After consideration of all the evidence, I consider that the risk assessments undertaken are suitable and sufficient and that the training put in place addresses those risks in accordance with Regulation 4(1)(b) (ii) The Manual Handling Operations Regulations 1992.

40. The claimant's claim therefore fails on breach of statutory duty.

Points to Note

1. Manual Handling cases are often going to focus on the issue of risk assessments and training.

2. Consider in detail the Defendant's risk assessments for Manual Handling at an early stage, together with training records. If the Claimant had been trained in Manual Handling techniques, but not adopted the techniques and the risk assessments had addressed the risk, then the case is likely to fail.

3. The stronger manual handling cases are likely to be those where there are no adequate risk assessments or no risk assessments are all, or the Claimant has received no manual handling training.

4. However, be aware of generic manual handling risk assessments, it is arguable that the risk assessments must address the specific task in question.

5. Remember that post ERRA cases, proof of negligence will be required, but the 1992 Regulations will be a good guide as to the standard of care, and thus the Regulations should always be pleaded.

6. The medical expert must link causation of injury to breach of duty i.e. the injury was caused by manual handling.

7. The Court is likely to focus upon what steps the Defendant took to reduce the risk of manual handling activities to the lowest possible level. For example, could equipment have been provided to reduce a repetitive activity?

A Case that succeeded?

AILEEN COOPER v BRIGHT HORIZONS FAMILY SOLU-TIONS LTD (2013) was a manual handling case that succeeded. The facts from the Judgment were as follows:-

1. *This action arises out on an incident which took place on 2nd June 2009 whilst Mrs Cooper was working as a Nursery Nurse for Bright Horizons Family Solutions Limited ("the Defendant") at the Rothampsted Little Stars Nursery, Harpenden. Mrs Cooper was working in the baby room and had placed a baby in a cot when she experienced back pain.*

4. *Mrs Cooper is a Nursery Nurse, who had obtained her qualification after the youngest of her three children went to nursery. She began working for the Defendant as a full-time Nursery Nurse on 2nd January 2008.*

5. *A copy of the Defendant's Job Description has been made available, which includes, under a section relevant to manual handling, the following passage: "Physical demands - Ensure children's safety while performing the following job functions – Frequently lift, move or hold children with a range of weight from 5 kg – 20 kg (Occasionally lift, move or hold weight more than 20 kg) ... Demonstrate full range of motion to lift, reach, squat, climb sit and otherwise fully participate in activities."*

6. *The Defendant's Handbook also requested a health declaration on taking up employment. Mrs Cooper's Health Declaration Form in answer to the question "Have you had any major injury within the last five years? Stated "Yes" "Back problem". It also disclosed that she was undergoing "physio". Later in the same declaration she*

ticked the box as to whether that she had problems with her back, neck, arms, legs and joints. She also disclosed she had been receiving ongoing physiotherapy since 8th December 2007. The induction sign-off sheet, which was completed on 2nd June 2008, indicated that Mrs Cooper had seen the induction video.

8. *The age group of the children at the nursery ranged from 18 months to 2 1/2 years but there was also facility for babies from about the age of four months. Mrs Cooper was transferred to the baby room in January 2009 after various members of the staff had left the Defendant's employment. The plan was that she would be employed in that capacity for three months until new staff had arrived.*

9. *There were five cots in the sleeping room, three with drop down sides which at one stage operated with a drop down mechanism. One of the issues in the case is whether the mechanism was broken or whether the plastic ties on the cot sides were fixed solely to prevent the sides being dropped down. The other two cots were not drop down cots and their bases were slightly higher. Mrs Cooper said that it was necessary to lean over and extend her arms to put a baby down or pick a baby up. She recollects that the mechanism for dropping the sides was broken, and this had been mentioned to various different managers and senior staff. She says that she had mentioned the defect to Ms Macer when Ms Macer started to work as a manager at the nursery.*

10. *Mrs Cooper's recollection is that the only training she received from the Defendant was an instruction to bend her knees when lifting items off the floor. At the time she received that training she was working in the pre-school area and was not concerned with lifting babies. She had received training about changing nappies for babies. She says she did not receive any training concerning lifting babies into and out of cots.*

11. *Mrs Cooper says that on 2nd June 2009 she was working in the baby room when she lifted a six or seven month old baby into a*

cot. She believes that the baby was of normal size, tall but not overly heavy. The cot was one on which the mechanism was broken and the side would not drop down. She held him close to her body, went right up to the cot, almost leaning on it, in order to put him down on the mattress. She was unable to bend her legs as the cot side was too high. Mrs Cooper is 5' 6" tall. She had to be close to the side of the cot in order to reach down. As she was about to put him on the mattress, she felt her back go. She described it as "a sharp pulling pain". She says that as she stood by the cot soothing the baby her "back had become incredibly painful". She described her legs as not feeling right and used the side of the cot to steady herself.

12. Mrs Cooper went to fetch a plastic chair from the changing room, where her colleague, Ms Richmond, was at the time. Mrs Cooper says that she informed her that she had hurt her back and needed to sit down. She placed the chair next to the cot approximately level with the mattress. She placed her left arm over the side of the cot to sooth the baby. Her armpit was resting on the side of the cot. Although she does not know the depth of the cot, she was able to reach over and sooth the baby without her bottom leaving the chair. As she lowered her arm close to the baby "something felt like it had snapped in my back". She believes she was trying to look at the baby at the same time as reaching her arm into the cot to sooth him. She therefore twisted her back without realising it. Mrs Cooper says that she was aware of "a much more excruciating and sharp pain in her back". Her legs were heavy and became numb.

13. Mrs Cooper describes sitting on the chair for about five minutes before hobbling into the main room to speak to a colleague. She managed to stay at work for the rest of the day in agony. She went to work the following day with increasing pain before attending her General Practitioner who prescribed further pain killers. Over the weekend she began to develop urinary incontinence and attended her General Practitioner again on 8th June 2009, who referred her to hospital with a suspected cauda equina syndrome. Mrs Cooper underwent surgery from which she has made only a partial

recovery. She did not return to work. Mrs Cooper believes that the cots were not replaced or repaired until sometime in December 2009.

The Court found in relation to the 1992 Regulations:-

46. *I am also satisfied that there was a breach of regulation 4 of The Manual Handling Operations Regulations 1992. The requirement under Regulation 4(1) (a), as set out in full above, is that each employer shall "so far as is reasonably practicable, avoid the need for his employers to undertake any manual handling operations at work which involve a risk of their being injured." In my view, Regulation 4 was engaged in this case because there was a real and foreseeable risk of injury to Mrs Cooper undertaking the manoeuvre she has described of putting the baby into the cot without her being able to put the cot side down.*

47. *I n Koonjul v Thameslink Healthcare Services [2000] PIQR P123 Hale LJ said at paras 9 to 13:*

*"9. Mr Weir also complains that the risk of injury need not be significant. He refers to the one case (as far as we know) in which these regulations have previously been considered by this court, the case of **Hawkes v London Borough of Southwark** (unreported transcript 20th February 1998). In that case, Aldous LJ referred to their having to be a "real" risk for the purpose of the regulations. Mr Weir refers also to the Scottish case of **Cullen v North Lanarkshire Council [1998] SC 451 at 455**, where the court referred to the risk of injury needing to be "no more than a foreseeable possibility; it need not be a probability."*

*10. For my part, I am quite prepared to accept those statements as to the level of risk which is required to **bring the case within the obligations of regulation 4; that there must be a real risk, a foreseeable possibility of injury; certainly nothing approaching a probability.** I am also prepared to accept that, in making an assessment of whether* *there is such a risk of injury, the employer is not entitled to assume that all his employees will on all occasions behave with full and proper concern for their own safety. I accept that the purpose of regulations such as these is indeed to place upon employers' obligations to look after their employees' safety which they might not otherwise have.*

11. However, in making such assessments there has to be an element of realism. As the guidance on the regulations points out, in appendix 1 at paragraph 3: . . . a full assessment of every manual handling operation could be a major undertaking and might involve wasted effort."

13. It then goes on to give numerical guidelines for the purpose of providing "an initial filter which can help to identify those manual handling operations deserving more detailed examination."

14. It also seems to me clear to be that the question of what does involve a risk of injury must be context-based. One is therefore looking at this particular operation in the context of this particular place of employment and also the particular employees involved. *In this case, we have a small residential home with a small number of employees. But those employees were carrying out what may be regarded as everyday tasks, and this particular employee had been carrying out such tasks for a very long time indeed. The employer in seeking to assess the risks is entitled to take that into account."*

50.   The result of the Defendant's own risk assessment for "Lifting Babies and toddlers" identified a medium level of risk for staff with known back problems. The specific assessment for use of cots identified a high level of risk in respect of holding loads away from the body, and a medium level of risk in relation to twisting. **In my view, the risk was avoidable by being able to drop the cot side down. Moreover, I find that Mrs Cooper did not receive training on lifting babies or small children, by training video or otherwise.**

51.   It does not seem to me that the Defendant can now resile from the risk assessment that was actually undertaken and now rely upon the

*submission that it was wrong. As Hale LJ said in **Koonjul v Thameslink Healthcare Services (supra), the question of what does involve a risk of injury must be context-based.** Although lifting and putting down babies in cots may, in the context of ordinary life be an everyday activity, in the context of a nursery it is necessary for the Defendant to have developed procedures for doing so, a fact which it recognised in its own assessment. From the outset of Mrs Cooper's employment, as is evident from the statement on the Health Declaration Form, the Defendant was aware of Mrs Cooper's pre- existing back condition and did not follow its own guidance for employees with bad backs. The experts are agreed that the average weight of a six month old baby would be 7.26 kgs which was larger than the weight at shoulder height shown in the guidance.*

52. *For the avoidance of doubt I also consider that the risk assessment should have included the situation where babies are soothed whilst Nursery Nurses are sitting on the chair next to the cot, in particular the inadvisability of stretching their arms over the side of the cot. In doing so Mrs Cooper twisted her body and caused further damage to a major prolapsed disc. I note that Mrs Parr, when conducting the same manoeuvre, placed her arm through the sides of the cot rather than over the side.*

Points to Consider:-

1. The risk as in *Koonjul* must be context based. The case stated "**One is therefore looking at this particular operation in the context of this particular place of employment and also the particular employees involved**". Therefore, the risk assessment must be specific.

2. Further, the case highlights that to bring a case under Regulation 4 (or in negligence pot ERRA), the "**that there must be a real risk, a foreseeable possibility of injury; certainly nothing approaching a probability**".

3. The case above succeeded because the risk assessment was inadequate for the particular task in question, and because there was a lack of training. Again these are likely to be the key issues to consider in any manual handling case.

CHAPTER NINE
ACCIDENTS ON CONSTRUCTION
SITES: THE CONSTRUCTION DESIGN
AND MANAGEMENT REGULATIONS
2015, LIABILITY OF INDEPENDENT
CONTRACTORS, KEY CASES
AND PROVING NEGLIGENCE

Construction site accidents make up a significant number of Employer's Liability Claims, and thus, are deserving of a chapter of their own.

Construction Design and Management Regulations 2015

The Regulations set out as follows:-

Client duties in relation to managing projects
4.—(1) A client must make suitable arrangements for managing a project, including the allocation of sufficient time and other resources.
(2) Arrangements are suitable if they ensure that—
(a) the construction work can be carried out, so far as is reasonably practicable, without risks to the health or safety of any person affected by the project; and
(b) the facilities required by Schedule 2 are provided in respect of any person carrying out construction work.
(3) A client must ensure that these arrangements are maintained and reviewed throughout the project.
(4) A client must provide pre-construction information as soon as is practicable to every designer and contractor appointed, or being considered for appointment, to the project.
(5) A client must ensure that—
(a) before the construction phase begins, a construction phase plan is drawn up by the contractor if there is only one contractor, or by the principal contractor; and

(b) the principal designer prepares a health and safety file for the project, which—

(i) complies with the requirements of regulation 12(5);

(ii) is revised from time to time as appropriate to incorporate any relevant new information; and

(iii) is kept available for inspection by any person who may need it to comply with any relevant legal requirements.

(6) A client must take reasonable steps to ensure that—

(a) the principal designer complies with any other principal designer duties in regulations 11 and 12; and

(b) the principal contractor complies with any other principal contractor duties in regulations 12 to 14.

(7) If a client disposes of the client's interest in the structure, the client complies with the duty in paragraph (5)(b)(iii) by providing the health and safety file to the person who acquires the client's interest in the structure and ensuring that that person is aware of the nature and purpose of the file.

(8) Where there is more than one client in relation to a project—

(a) one or more of the clients may agree in writing to be treated for the purposes of these Regulations as the only client or clients; and

(b) except for the duties specified in sub-paragraph (c) only the client or clients agreed in paragraph (a) are subject to the duties owed by a client under these Regulations;

(c) the duties in the following provisions are owed by all clients—

(i) regulation 8(4); and

(ii) paragraph (4) and regulation 8(6) to the extent that those duties relate to information in the possession of the client.

Appointment of the principal designer and the principal contractor
5.—(1) Where there is more than one contractor, or if it is reasonably foreseeable that more than one contractor will be working on a project at any time, the client must appoint in writing—

(a) a designer with control over the pre-construction phase as principal designer; and

(b) a contractor as principal contractor.

(2) The appointments must be made as soon as is practicable, and, in any event, before the construction phase begins.

(3) If the client fails to appoint a principal designer, the client must fulfil the duties of the principal designer in regulation 11 and 12.

(4) If the client fails to appoint a principal contractor, the client must fulfil the duties of the principal contractor in regulations 12 to 14.

General duties

8.—(1) A designer (including a principal designer) or contractor (including a principal contractor) appointed to work on a project must have the skills, knowledge and experience, and, if they are an organisation, the organisational capability, necessary to fulfil the role that they are appointed to undertake, in a manner that secures the health and safety of any person affected by the project.

(2) A designer or contractor must not accept an appointment to a project unless they fulfil the conditions in paragraph (1).

(3) A person who is responsible for appointing a designer or contractor to carry out work on a project must take reasonable steps to satisfy themselves that the designer or contractor fulfils the conditions in paragraph (1).

(4) A person with a duty or function under these Regulations must cooperate with any other person working on or in relation to a project, at the same or an adjoining construction site, to the extent necessary to enable any person with a duty or function to fulfil that duty or function.

(5) A person working on a project under the control of another must report to that person anything they are aware of in relation to the project which is likely to endanger their own health or safety or that of others.

(6) Any person who is required by these Regulations to provide information or instruction must ensure the information or instruction is comprehensible and provided as soon as is practicable.

(7) To the extent that they are applicable to a domestic client, the duties in paragraphs (3), (4) and (6) must be carried out by the person specified in regulation 7(1).

Duties of a principal designer in relation to health and safety at the pre-construction phase

11.—(1) The principal designer must plan, manage and monitor the pre-construction phase and coordinate matters relating to health and safety during the pre-construction phase to ensure that, so far as is reasonably practicable, the project is carried out without risks to health or safety.

(2) In fulfilling the duties in paragraph (1), and in particular when—

(a) design, technical and organisational aspects are being decided in order to plan the various items or stages of work which are to take place simultaneously or in succession; and

(b) estimating the period of time required to complete such work or work stages, the principal designer must take into account the general principles of prevention and, where relevant, the content of any construction phase plan and any health and safety file.

(3) In fulfilling the duties in paragraph (1), the principal designer must identify and eliminate or control, so far as is reasonably practicable, foreseeable risks to the health or safety of any person—

(a) carrying out or liable to be affected by construction work;

(b) maintaining or cleaning a structure; or

(c) using a structure designed as a workplace.

(4) In fulfilling the duties in paragraph (1), the principal designer must ensure all designers comply with their duties in regulation 9.

(5) In fulfilling the duty to coordinate health and safety matters in paragraph (1), the principal designer must ensure that all persons working in relation to the pre-construction phase cooperate with the client, the principal designer and each other.

(6) The principal designer must—

(a) assist the client in the provision of the pre-construction information required by regulation 4(4); and

(b) so far as it is within the principal designer's control, provide pre-construction information, promptly and in a convenient form, to every designer and contractor appointed, or being considered for appointment, to the project.

(7) The principal designer must liaise with the principal contractor for the duration of the principal designer's appointment and share with the principal contractor information relevant to the planning, management and monitoring of the construction phase and the

coordination of health and safety matters during the construction phase.

Construction phase plan and health and safety file

12.—(1) During the pre-construction phase, and before setting up a construction site, the principal contractor must draw up a construction phase plan, or make arrangements for a construction phase plan to be drawn up.

(2) The construction phase plan must set out the health and safety arrangements and site rules taking account, where necessary, of the industrial activities taking place on the construction site and, where applicable, must include specific measures concerning work which falls within one or more of the categories set out in Schedule 3.

(3) The principal designer must assist the principal contractor in preparing the construction phase plan by providing to the principal contractor all information the principal designer holds that is relevant to the construction phase plan including—

(a) pre-construction information obtained from the client;

(b) any information obtained from designers under regulation 9(3)(b).

(4) Throughout the project the principal contractor must ensure that the construction phase plan is appropriately reviewed, updated and revised from time to time so that it continues to be sufficient to ensure that construction work is carried out, so far as is reasonably practicable, without risks to health or safety.

(5) During the pre-construction phase, the principal designer must prepare a health and safety file appropriate to the characteristics of the project which must contain information relating to the project which is likely to be needed during any subsequent project to ensure the health and safety of any person.

(6) The principal designer must ensure that the health and safety file is appropriately reviewed, updated and revised from time to time to take account of the work and any changes that have occurred.

(7) During the project, the principal contractor must provide the principal designer with any information in the principal contractor's possession relevant to the health and safety file, for inclusion in the health and safety file.

(8) If the principal designer's appointment concludes before the end of the project, the principal designer must pass the health and safety file to the principal contractor.

(9) Where the health and safety file is passed to the principal contractor under paragraph (8), the principal contractor must ensure that the health and safety file is appropriately reviewed, updated and revised from time to time to take account of the work and any changes that have occurred.

(10) At the end of the project, the principal designer, or where there is no principal designer the principal contractor, must pass the health and safety file to the client.

Duties of a principal contractor in relation to health and safety at the construction phase

13.—(1) The principal contractor must plan, manage and monitor the construction phase and coordinate matters relating to health and safety during the construction phase to ensure that, so far as is reasonably practicable, construction work is carried out without risks to health or safety.

(2) In fulfilling the duties in paragraph (1), and in particular when—

(a) design, technical and organisational aspects are being decided in order to plan the various items or stages of work which are to take place simultaneously or in succession; and

(b) estimating the period of time required to complete the work or work stages, the principal contractor must take into account the general principles of prevention.

(3) The principal contractor must—

(a) organise cooperation between contractors (including successive contractors on the same construction site);

(b) coordinate implementation by the contractors of applicable legal requirements for health and safety; and

(c) ensure that employers and, if necessary for the protection of workers, self-employed persons—

(i) apply the general principles of prevention in a consistent manner, and in particular when complying with the provisions of Part 4; and

(ii) where required, follow the construction phase plan.

(4) The principal contractor must ensure that—

(a) a suitable site induction is provided;

(b) the necessary steps are taken to prevent access by unauthorised persons to the construction site; and

(c) facilities that comply with the requirements of Schedule 2 are provided throughout the construction phase.

(5) The principal contractor must liaise with the principal designer for the duration of the principal designer's appointment and share with the principal designer information relevant to the planning, management and monitoring of the pre-construction phase and the coordination of health and safety matters during the pre-construction phase.

Principal contractor's duties to consult and engage with workers
14. The principal contractor must—

(a) make and maintain arrangements which will enable the principal contractor and workers engaged in construction work to cooperate effectively in developing, promoting and checking the effectiveness of measures to ensure the health, safety and welfare of the workers;

(b) consult those workers or their representatives in good time on matters connected with the project which may affect their health, safety or welfare, in so far as they or their representatives have not been similarly consulted by their employer;

(c) ensure that those workers or their representatives can inspect and take copies of any information which the principal contractor has, or which these Regulations require to be provided to the principal contractor, which relate to the health, safety or welfare of workers at the site, except any information—

(i) the disclosure of which would be against the interests of national security;

(ii) which the principal contractor could not disclose without contravening a prohibition imposed by or under an enactment;

(iii) relating specifically to an individual, unless that individual has consented to its being disclosed;

(iv) the disclosure of which would, for reasons other than its effect on health, safety or welfare at work, cause substantial injury to the principal contractor's undertaking or, where the information was supplied

to the principal contractor by another person, to the undertaking of that other person;

(v) obtained by the principal contractor for the purpose of bringing, prosecuting or defending any legal proceedings.

Duties of contractors
15.—(1) A contractor must not carry out construction work in relation to a project unless satisfied that the client is aware of the duties owed by the client under these Regulations.

(2) A contractor must plan, manage and monitor construction work carried out either by the contractor or by workers under the contractor's control, to ensure that, so far as is reasonably practicable, it is carried out without risks to health and safety.

(3) Where there is more than one contractor working on a project, a contractor must comply with—

(a) any directions given by the principal designer or the principal contractor; and

(b) the parts of the construction phase plan that are relevant to that contractor's work on the project.

(4) If there is only one contractor working on the project, the contractor must take account of the general principles of prevention when—

(a) design, technical and organisational aspects are being decided in order to plan the various items or stages of work which are to take place simultaneously or in succession; and

(b) estimating the period of time required to complete the work or work stages.

(5) If there is only one contractor working on the project, the contractor must draw up a construction phase plan, or make arrangements for a construction phase plan to be drawn up, as soon as is practicable prior to setting up a construction site.

(6) The construction phase plan must fulfil the requirements of regulation 12(2).

(7) A contractor must not employ or appoint a person to work on a construction site unless that person has, or is in the process of obtaining, the necessary skills, knowledge, training and experience to carry out the tasks allocated to that person in a manner that secures the health and safety of any person working on the construction site.

(8) A contractor must provide each worker under their control with appropriate supervision, instructions and information so that construction work can be carried out, so far as is reasonably practicable, without risks to health and safety.

(9) The information provided must include—

(a) a suitable site induction, where not already provided by the principal contractor;

(b) the procedures to be followed in the event of serious and imminent danger to health and safety;

(c) information on risks to health and safety—

(i) identified by the risk assessment under regulation 3 of the Management Regulations; or

(ii) arising out of the conduct of another contractor's undertaking and of which the contractor in control of the worker ought reasonably to be aware; and

(d) any other information necessary to enable the worker to comply with the relevant statutory provisions.

(10) A contractor must not begin work on a construction site unless reasonable steps have been taken to prevent access by unauthorised persons to that site.

(11) A contractor must ensure, so far as is reasonably practicable, that the requirements of Schedule 2 are complied with so far as they affect the contractor or any worker under that contractor's control.

Points to Note

1. The Regulations are likely to apply to the main contractor and sub contractor. In a construction site accident claim, it is extremely important to consider who had control of the site and consider the potential liability of the main contractor and any sub contractors. The starting point is likely to be, who engaged the Claimant.

2. The CDM regulations (especially 13 and 14 replacing Regulations 23 and 34 under the 2007 Regulations) are a useful guide as to the standards of care upon the principal contractor for site safety. Even if the Claimant was not employed or engaged by

the principal contractor, one should always consider whether the principal contractor has complied with Regulations 13 and 14 in particular.

3. If various sub contractors blame each other, it may be necessary to consider adding multiple Defendants to the proceedings and seeking a Sanderson/Bullock order as to costs. It is not unusual for construction site accidents to result in multiple Defendant cases, where a main contractor and a number of sub contractors have been involved.

A Case in Point

The Regulations were considered in *DAVID MIDDLETON v (1) RAYMOND MOORE (T/A R MOORE CONSTRUCTION & AGRI-CULTURAL ENGINEERS) (2) DEREK MOORE (3) ROBERT HOWELL (2012)* and the facts were as follows:-

4. *The Third Defendant has three farms, one of which is White Horse Farm, Scarning, Norfolk. In 2008 he decided to demolish inter alia three square silos in a barn. The silos had walls consisting of corrugated steel panels. The panels were to be re-used to extend another barn. To carry out the work he engaged the First Defendant, who traded as a construction and agricultural engineer, and who had carried out construction work for him on many occasions in the past. The First Defendant instructed the Claimant, the Second Defendant and Keith Robinson to do the work. The Claimant had worked for the First Defendant 4 days per week for some 3 years prior to the accident. The Second Defendant worked for the First Defendant on average about two to three days per week. Keith Robinson had worked for the First Defendant five days a week since January 2007, the hours he worked depending on a school taxi contract he had. During their time working for the First Defendant they had worked at the Third Defendant's farms on about 3 occasions.*

5. *The panels forming the sides of the square silos were bolted horizontally in units of 5 panels. Each panel measured 10' long by 3' wide, so that a unit of 5 panels measured about 10' by 15' overall and weighed about 800 lbs. Each silo was of the order of 15 to 20 feet high.*

6. *The work began approximately two weeks prior to the Claimant's accident. A five panel unit was unbolted, removed in one piece slung from a teleporter owned by the Third Defendant, dragged outside the barn and then laid flat on the ground. I was told by the Second Defendant, and I accept, that removing this 5 panel unit had not been easy. Other panels were removed individually, each one being slung from the teleporter. The teleporter had a working platform, also described as a "cage" and "bucket". To gain access to the sheets on top, typically the First Defendant would lie on the platform floor, reach down and undo the nuts with a powered "nut runner" whilst the Claimant stood on a ladder on the opposite side of the sheet, holding the bolt's nut with a spanner. On such occasions Robinson drove the teleporter.*

7. *The accident happened when the Claimant and the First Defendant had to unbolt the individual panels from the 5 panel unit which had already been removed and laid on the ground outside. Given that the unit had been laid flat on the ground, it had to be raised to enable access to both sides at the same time to enable the bolts to be freed. How that was done is very much in issue.*

8. *The Claimant's case is that the Second Defendant decided to use the teleporter and sling the unit (also described in evidence as "the sheets" and "the walling") from the teleporter, that the Second Defendant gave him a rope sling which he attached to the unit and the Second Defendant, driving the teleporter, lifted the unit so that it rested on the ground at an angle. He says that the Second Defendant then addressed the bolt heads on the upper side of the sheets and on the instructions of the Second Defendant he went on the underside to hold the bolt nuts with a spanner. When he was*

underneath the sheets the rope broke and the unit fell trapping him underneath.

9. *The Second Defendant denies this account. He says that he and the Claimant between them decided to and did lift one end of the 5 sheet unit and put wooden props under the corners at the raised end, so that the raised end was about 2' above ground level, He says the Claimant then went underneath the sheets and that when he, the Second Defendant, was operating the nut runner the unit slipped on the props and fell trapping the Claimant underneath".*

The case was dismissed on the basis of unreliable evidence from the Claimant but the Court did consider the relevance of the CDM Regulations 2007:-

Under CDMR
(i) On every contractor carrying out construction work to comply with regulations ?6-44 insofar as affect him or any person carrying out construction work under his control or relating to matters within his control
(Ree 2s(1)).
31 On every person (other than a contractor) who controls the way in which any construction work is carried out to comply with regulations 26-44 insofar as they relate to matters within his control (Reg 25(2).
Regulation 26 imposes the obligation to make and keep safe places of work.
Regulation 29 imposes the obligation to plan and carry out demolition or dismantling of a structure in such a manner as to prevent danger, or where it is not practicable to prevent it, to reduce danger to as low a level as reasonably practicable.

I would have held the First Defendant, as the Claimant's employer and as a person who was controlling the Claimant's work to have been in breach of Regulations 4(Ll, and 5(1) of PUWER ; of Regulations 4 and 8 of LOLER ; of Regulation 3 of MHSWR; and, as a contractor, in breach of Regulations 26 and 29 of CDMR.

I would have held that the rope sling had been provided with the teleporter by the Third Defendant and that the Third Defendant had sufficient control of the teleporter and equipment supplied with it to be subject to PUWER and LOLER and that he had been in breach of Regulations 4(L), and 5(1) of PUWER and of Regulations 4 and 8 of LOLER. There is no need to consider the other allegations made against him.

I would have found that the Second Defendant did not have control *within PUWER, LOLER* **and CDMR***. I would however have found that the Second Defendant and the Claimant were acting jointly, should not have used the rope for lifting the unit and that the decision that the Claimant would go underneath the sheets was consciously or otherwise arrived at jointly with neither considering sufficiently whether or not it was safe, which it was not, to do so. So far as the Second Defendant was negligent, the First Defendant as his employer would also be liable vicariously for that negligence. So far as the Claimant was negligent, that would reflect itself in a finding of contributory negligence"*

RONALD KEITH MCCOOK v (1) ALOYSIUS LOBO (2) LONDON SEAFOOD LTD (3) STANLEY HEADLEY (2002) was another case which looked at the 1994 CDM Regulations which contain similar provision to the updated 2007 and 2015 Regulations (now in force):-

Start of construction phase
10. Every client shall ensure, so far as is reasonably practicable, that the construction phase of any project does not start unless a **health and safety plan complying with regulation 15(4) has been prepared in respect of that project.**

The facts were as follows:-

1. *On 7th July 1995, Mr Chinery, the claimant, suffered severe injury resulting in paraplegia when he fell down a 700 mm circular capped ventilation duct from the seventh floor south mechanical*

riser room at St George's House, Wimbledon. The accident occurred when he was working as an employee of Engineering with Excellence Limited, the first defendant appellant, as a lagger. The circumstances of this unfortunate accident were most unusual.

2. *The main contractors for the refurbishment of this office block were Laing South East Limited. Balfour Kilpatrick Limited, the second defendants, were sub-contractors to Laing for the mechanical and public health works. This included installing a new air-conditioning system, which required pipe work, duct work, lagging and electrical works. Zeldatree Limited, the third defendants, were specialist duct work sub-sub-contractors to Balfour Kilpatrick Ltd. The first defendants were sub-contractors to Balfour Kilpatrick whose work included carrying out insulation work to newly installed chilled water pipe work.*

3. *The seventh floor riser room contained two circular air-conditioning ducts, one of 700 mm in diameter and the other rather larger, approximately 900 mm in diameter. The smaller one of these was redundant. Its space was required for other new works. About two days before Mr Chinery's accident, or thereabouts, Mr Ian Rae, the second defendants' site manager, asked Gary Paul, a duct work fitter employed by the third defendants who were working on the site, to remove some ducts from the riser cupboard on the seventh floor so that they could get the new pipes in. Mr Rae originally asked Mr Paul to remove the 700 mm duct at floor level, but this was not practical. So Mr Rae agreed that it should be cut down to what Gary Paul described as "waist height". This was some 700 mm to 900 mm above the floor level. The judge found that it was 700 mm, or thereabouts, above floor level. Gary Paul and two other of the third defendants' fitters accordingly removed the duct leaving it at about waist height. Gary Paul did not give oral evidence, but his statement to the Health and Safety Executive was put in by the first defendants under the Civil Evidence Act. He said in this witness statement that he did not think that anyone would be going into the cupboard so he left the duct open after he had finishing reducing it in height and had shut the cupboard.*

Later he was asked by someone from the second defendants, he thought it was Ian Rae, to ask Paul Bloomfield, the third defendants' designer, to get a capping end for the duct. Ian Rae said that the cap end was to suit the spiral duct to stop dust going down it. He did not say that anyone would need to stand on it. No-one told him, that is Mr Paul, that this might happen. Paul Bloomfield came to measure for the end cap. Gary Paul's statement indicates that he was aware that additional pipe work was being installed in the riser room. When Gary Paul left the duct at the height it was there was nothing else in the cupboard that suggested that anyone would need to stand on the cap end to get to it. There was no other evidence from the third defendants.

4. *The duct itself was made of spirally wound galvanised mild steel sheet 1 mm or slightly less thick. The cap to the end was of similar specification. It sat on a lip and was rivetted to the wall of the spiral duct. We have seen either it, or an example of it, brought into court. Each of the ducts and the cap complied with HVCA duct work specification DW142. The cap was intended as a dust cap. It was not intended to be stood on. Nor is it clear that the duct itself would have been load-bearing if the cap alone had been strengthened. Ducts manufactured to DW142 are not expected to have structural stability to support the weight of a man. If it is thought that ducts will be stood on, it is normal to construct some-thing in the nature of a small gantry.*

5. *Mr Chinery was installing lagging to chilled water air-conditioning pipes at a high level in this riser room. To do this he was standing, somewhat precariously no doubt for some time, on the angle of some existing pipe work. As he was descending to get to the floor, he stood on the cap of the reduced ventilation duct. Having suffered severe injuries he was not able to give exact details of how it happened; but the cap was incapable of carrying his weight and he fell through it from the seventh floor nearly to the first floor. He brought pro-ceedings for personal injury against the first, second and third defendants.*

The Court found that while the first and second defendants had breached Reg.10 Construction (Design and Management) Regulations 1994, that breach was not causative of injuries sustained by the Claimant when he fell from a ladder on a construction site. It said:-

25. *In my judgment no point of principle arises in this case.* **As I said in my judgment in the Plant case, the extent of a contractor's or sub-contractor's responsibility to warn of dangers on a construction site depends on all the relevant circumstances.** *Here Mr Rae, the second defendants' senior project manager, instructed Mr Paul, who was a fitter, to arrange for the duct to be capped. As a matter of fact, it seems to me that the lawyer's question is the same as the question on the ground, that is whether in all the circumstances Mr Paul should have given a warning or whether Mr Bloomfield, the third defendants' designer, should have either given a warning or designed something different. Mr Rae knew what was going to happen in the riser room subsequently. Mr Paul and Mr Bloomfield did not, other than by supposition. Critically, to my mind, Mr Paul was a fitter with no supervisory function. He should, I think, in the circumstances of this case, be regarded as in a position of an operative of the second defendants. Mr Bloomfield was a designer, and it is to be supposed that it was he who decided how in detail capping should be done. Although it is accepted that the material from which the cap was made was not explicitly specified (in that the choice made was suitable for a dust cover), the evidence appears to indicate that the choice was made probably by the third defendants, presumably by Mr Bloomfield, and further that he designed the detailed way in which that cover was to be fixed. It seems to me that the evidence of Mr Gosnell should be accepted as referable to Mr Bloomfield, if not to Mr Paul, to the effect that the third defendants would in general terms be aware that it was highly probable that at some point in the life of the installation someone would stand on the capped end of the duct.* **The third defendants through Mr Bloomfield have something of a contractual design responsibility, but in my judgment he was not obliged unilaterally to decide to design something fundamentally different from what he had been asked to design.** *The*

highest that it could be put is that he was obliged to appreciate and warn that what he had designed would not support a man's weight and that steps of some kind should be taken to guard against the kind of accident which in fact unfortunately happened.

28. *As between the second and third defendants, I think that the responsibility for seeing that the room with its capped duct was safe for laggers lay entirely with the second defendant - one at least of these engineers inspected and approved the work - and that a claim by the claimant against the third defendants would fail. Although the risk that someone might tread on the capped duct may, in the view of an expert, have been foreseeable, I consider that in this case the third defendants were in the position of a sub-contractor who did was what asked of them but who had no obligation to see that further steps were taken by others, in particular the second defendant. The second defendants were themselves in control of the use of the room; they knew that the duct capped was not strong enough to be stood on; and they themselves had the responsibility with the first defendants for ensuring that the claimant could safely use the room".*

The cases highlight as follows:-

a) Principal Contractors and Sub Contractors can have duties under the CDM Regulations.

b) In post ERRA 2013 cases, it will be necessary still to show breach of the common law duty of care. The CDM Regulations themselves will not give rise to a cause of action in themselves, but again may be a useful guide to the likely standards of care for Principal Contractors and Sub Contractors in relation to construction site claims.

c) In relation the application of the CDM Regulations the element of some form of control of the site or work is key to prove negligence against a Defendant. In

Middleton it was stated by the Court that "*I would have held the First Defendant, as the Claimant's employer and as a person who was controlling the Claimant's work and, as a contractor, in breach of Regulations 26 and 29 of CDMR*". *McCook* also emphasised the same point of control "*The second defendants were themselves in control of the use of the room; they knew that the duct capped was not strong enough to be stood on; and they themselves had the responsibility with the first defendants for ensuring that the claimant could safely use the room*".

CHAPTER TEN
ACCIDENTS INVOLVING WORK EQUIPMENT: THE PROVISION AND USE OF WORK EQUIPMENT REGULATIONS 1998, KEY CASES AND PROVING NEGLIGENCE

There are a number of relevant Regulations that can be pleaded and utilised in pre section 69 ERRA cases (see earlier chapters regarding the Enterprise Act).

Application of the 1998 Work Equipment Regulations

3.—(1) These Regulations shall apply—
(a) in Great Britain; and
(b) outside Great Britain as sections 1 to 59 and 80 to 82 of the 1974 Act apply by virtue of the Health and Safety at Work etc. Act 1974 (Application outside Great Britain) Order 1995(1) ("the 1995 Order").
(2) The requirements imposed by these Regulations on an employer in respect of work equipment shall apply to such equipment provided for use or used by an employee of his at work.
(3) The requirements imposed by these Regulations on an employer shall also apply—
(a) to a self-employed person, in respect of work equipment he uses at work;
(b) subject to paragraph (5), to a person who has control to any extent of—
(i) work equipment;
(ii) a person at work who uses or supervises or manages the use of work equipment; or
(iii) the way in which work equipment is used at work,
and to the extent of his control.
(4) Any reference in paragraph (3)(b) to a person having control is a reference to a person having control in connection with the carrying on

by him of a trade, business or other undertaking (whether for profit or not).

Common Citations

The most commonly cited Regulations relate to suitability, maintenance and inspection, of Work Equipment:-

Suitability of work equipment
4.—(1) Every employer shall ensure that work equipment is so constructed or adapted as to be suitable for the purpose for which it is used or provided.

(2) In selecting work equipment, every employer shall have regard to the working conditions and to the risks to the health and safety of persons which exist in the premises or undertaking in which that work equipment is to be used and any additional risk posed by the use of that work equipment.

(3) Every employer shall ensure that work equipment is used only for operations for which, and under conditions for which, it is suitable.

(4) In this regulation "suitable" means suitable in any respect which it is reasonably foreseeable will affect the health or safety of any person.

Maintenance
5.—(1) Every employer shall ensure that work equipment is maintained in an efficient state, in efficient working order and in good repair.

(2) Every employer shall ensure that where any machinery has a maintenance log, the log is kept up to date.

Inspection
6.—(1) Every employer shall ensure that, where the safety of work equipment depends on the installation conditions, it is inspected—
(a) after installation and before being put into service for the first time; or
(b) after assembly at a new site or in a new location, to ensure that it has been installed correctly and is safe to operate.

(2) Every employer shall ensure that work equipment exposed to conditions causing deterioration which is liable to result in dangerous situations is inspected—

(a) at suitable intervals; and

(b) each time that exceptional circumstances which are liable to jeopardise the safety of the work equipment have occurred, to ensure that health and safety conditions are maintained and that any deterioration can be detected and remedied in good time.

(3) Every employer shall ensure that the result of an inspection made under this regulation is recorded and kept until the next inspection under this regulation is recorded.

(4) Every employer shall ensure that no work equipment—

(a) leaves his undertaking; or

(b) if obtained from the undertaking of another person, is used in his undertaking, unless it is accompanied by physical evidence that the last inspection required to be carried out under this regulation has been carried out.

(5) This regulation does not apply to—

(a) a power press to which regulations 32 to 35 apply;

(b) a guard or protection device for the tools of such power press;

(c) work equipment for lifting loads including persons;

(d) winding apparatus to which the Mines (Shafts and Winding) Regulations 1993(1) apply;

(e) work equipment required to be inspected by regulation 29 of the Construction (Health, Safety and Welfare) Regulations 1996(2).

HSE Guidance – Maintenance, Inspection and Suitability

The HSE guidance which can be found online at: http://www.hse.-gov.uk/pubns/indg291.pdf, also provides the following useful guidance to the applicability of the Regulations:-

You must ensure that the work equipment you provide meets the requirements of PUWER. You should ensure that it is:

- *suitable for use, and for the purpose and conditions in which it is to be used;*

- *maintained in a safe condition for use so that people's health and safety is not at risk; and*
- *inspected, in certain circumstances, to ensure that it is and continues to be safe for use. Any inspection should be carried out by a competent person (this could be an employee if they have the necessary skills, knowledge and experience to perform the task) and a record kept until the next inspection.*

You should also ensure that risks created by using the equipment are eliminated where possible or controlled as far as reasonably practicable by:

- *taking appropriate 'hardware' measures, eg providing suitable guards, protection devices, markings and warning devices, system control devices (such as emergency stop buttons) and personal protective equipment; and*
- *taking appropriate 'software' measures such as following safe systems of work (eg ensuring maintenance is only performed when equipment is shut down etc), and providing adequate information, instruction and training about the specific equipment.*

A combination of these measures may be necessary depending on the requirements of the work, your assessment of the risks involved, and the practicability of such measures.

The Main Case – Stark v Post Office

The main case of Stark sets out as follows, to show how in relation to pre Enterprise Act cases, the Regulations would impose strict liability in relation to defective work equipment cases:-

Mr Stark the appellant is 60 years of age. He was employed as a delivery postman by the Post Office the respondents. The Post Office provided him with a bicycle with which to make his deliveries. On 29th July 1994 in the course of his employment he was riding his bicycle along Padstow Close, Bransholme, Hull when without warning his front wheel locked and he was propelled over the handlebars and suffered serious injury. The accident was caused by the fact that the stirrup, part of the front brake, broke in two, and one part lodged in the front wheel.

The Post Office did in fact have a policy of replacing bicycles at 10 years, but this was not an inflexible rule. Sometimes, (as in the case of this bicycle) they thought this bicycle had a few years serviceable life left and allowed it to continue in service. This bicycle was in its 14th year. The judge found that if it had been replaced at 10 years the accident would have been prevented but did not suggest there was any fault on the part of the Post Office in taking the decision they did.

In the result His Honour Judge Cracknell found that there was no liability in negligence and from that finding there is no appeal.

The judge also found that there was no breach of statutory duty, and thus dismissed Mr Stark's claim. The regulations relied on by Mr Wood on behalf of Mr. Stark before the judge were regulations 5 and 6 of the Provision and Use of Work Equipment Regulations 1992. Before us Mr Redfern QC has not relied on regulation 5 and this appeal is concerned with the judge's ruling that regulation 6(1) was not breached by the Post Office. Regulation 6(1) is in the following terms:-

"Every employer shall ensure that work equipment is maintained in an efficient state, in efficient working order and in good repair."

It seems that the argument before the judge on behalf of the Post Office was that the regulation did not apply because the regulation was concerned with maintenance and not with replacement, and that if anything this was a replacement case. I am not sure the judge accepted that argument because at page 3 of his judgment he said:-

"On the face of the matter therefore it seems that this regulation may import strict liability into this part of the law. On the other hand, it seems to me the primary obligation is to institute and carry out a system of maintenance to the very best of their ability and this the Post Office did. At the risk of indulging in sophistry the visible state of the bicycle immediately prior to the event would have confirmed that fact."

Mr Redfern's argument is that regulation 6(1) imposes an absolute obligation. His argument is straightforward. Work equipment is defined as "any machinery, appliance, apparatus or tool and any assembly of components which, in order to achieve a common end, are arranged and controlled so that they function as a whole" (see regulation 2(1)). That definition includes a bicycle but may place some limit on Mr Storey's suggested "all-embracing". He submitted that "maintained in an efficient state, in efficient working order . . . " meant that the bicycle had to be kept in a state in which it worked efficiently at all times; the bicycle was not working efficiently when the stirrup broke; and that whatever the reason for it not working efficiently, the Post Office were in breach of the regulation.

He submitted that the wording used in regulation 6(1) had been construed as imposing such an absolute obligation when used in other regulations concerned with the safety of employees. He relied in particular on Galashiels Gas Co Ltd v Millar [1949] AC 275 and Hamilton v National Coal Board [1960] AC 633. In Galashiels the headnote reads:-

"By the Factories Act, 1937, s. 22, sub-s. 1: "Every hoist or lift shall be of good mechanical construction, sound material and adequate strength, and be -3- properly maintained." By s. 152, sub-s. 1, the expression "maintained" means "maintained in an efficient state, in efficient working order and in good repair."

By s. 22, sub-s. 1, an absolute and continuing obligation is imposed, so that proof of any failure in the mechanism of a hoist or lift establishes a breach of the statutory duty, even though it was impossible to anticipate that failure before the event or to explain it afterwards and even though all reasonable steps have been taken to provide a suitable hoist or lift and to maintain it properly."

The Court Concluded:-

The draftsman here has used language construed as imposing a strict obligation over many years in the context of the Health and Safety of employees. That language gives effect to the minimum obligations, but it also goes further. I cannot see that there is any discouragement of the implementation of a higher standard if the Member State chooses to impose it.

In the circumstances it seems to me that regulation 6(1) does impose an absolute obligation, and that accordingly since the bicycle was not in an efficient state or in efficient working order when the stirrup broke, the Post Office were in breach of their statutory duty.

In those circumstances I would allow the appeal and enter judgment for Mr Stark with damages to be assessed.

Other Essential Components of the 1998 Regulations

Specific risks
7.—(1) Where the use of work equipment is likely to involve a specific risk to health or safety, every employer shall ensure that—
(a) the use of that work equipment is restricted to those persons given the task of using it; and
(b) repairs, modifications, maintenance or servicing of that work equipment is restricted to those persons who have been specifically designated to perform operations of that description (whether or not also authorised to perform other operations).
(2) The employer shall ensure that the persons designated for the purposes of sub-paragraph (b) of paragraph (1) have received adequate training related to any operations in respect of which they have been so designated.

Information and instructions
8.—(1) Every employer shall ensure that all persons who use work equipment have available to them adequate health and safety information and, where appropriate, written instructions pertaining to the use of the work equipment.
(2) Every employer shall ensure that any of his employees who supervises or manages the use of work equipment has available to him adequate health and safety information and, where appropriate, written instructions pertaining to the use of the work equipment.

(3) Without prejudice to the generality of paragraphs (1) or (2), the information and instructions required by either of those paragraphs shall include information and, where appropriate, written instructions on—
(a) the conditions in which and the methods by which the work equipment may be used;
(b) foreseeable abnormal situations and the action to be taken if such a situation were to occur; and
(c) any conclusions to be drawn from experience in using the work equipment.
(4) Information and instructions required by this regulation shall be readily comprehensible to those concerned.

Training
9.—(1) Every employer shall ensure that all persons who use work equipment have received adequate training for purposes of health and safety, including training in the methods which may be adopted when using the work equipment, any risks which such use may entail and precautions to be taken.
(2) Every employer shall ensure that any of his employees who supervises or manages the use of work equipment has received adequate training for purposes of health and safety, including training in the methods which may be adopted when using the work equipment, any risks which such use may entail and precautions to be taken.

Dangerous parts of machinery
11.—(1) Every employer shall ensure that measures are taken in accordance with paragraph (2) which are effective—
(a) to prevent access to any dangerous part of machinery or to any rotating stock-bar; or
(b) to stop the movement of any dangerous part of machinery or rotating stock-bar before any part of a person enters a danger zone.
(2) The measures required by paragraph (1) shall consist of—
(a) the provision of fixed guards enclosing every dangerous part or rotating stock-bar where and to the extent that it is practicable to do so, but where or to the extent that it is not, then

(b) the provision of other guards or protection devices where and to the extent that it is practicable to do so, but where or to the extent that it is not, then

(c) the provision of jigs, holders, push-sticks or similar protection appliances used in conjunction with the machinery where and to the extent that it is practicable to do so, but where or to the extent that it is not, then

(d) the provision of information, instruction, training and supervision.

(3) All guards and protection devices provided under sub-paragraphs (a) or (b) of paragraph (2) shall—

(a) be suitable for the purpose for which they are provided;

(b) be of good construction, sound material and adequate strength;

(c) be maintained in an efficient state, in efficient working order and in good repair;

(d) not give rise to any increased risk to health or safety;

(e) not be easily bypassed or disabled;

(f) be situated at sufficient distance from the danger zone;

(g) not unduly restrict the view of the operating cycle of the machinery, where such a view is necessary;

(h) be so constructed or adapted that they allow operations necessary to fit or replace parts and for maintenance work, restricting access so that it is allowed only to the area where the work is to be carried out and, if possible, without having to dismantle the guard or protection device.

(4) All protection appliances provided under sub-paragraph (c) of paragraph (2) shall comply with sub-paragraphs (a) to (d) and (g) of paragraph (3).

(5) In this regulation—

"danger zone" means any zone in or around machinery in which a person is exposed to a risk to health or safety from contact with a dangerous part of machinery or a rotating stock-bar;

"stock-bar" means any part of a stock-bar which projects beyond the head-stock of a lathe.

Protection against specified hazards

12.—(1) Every employer shall take measures to ensure that the exposure of a person using work equipment to any risk to his health or safety from any hazard specified in paragraph (3) is either prevented, or, where that is not reasonably practicable, adequately controlled.

(2) The measures required by paragraph (1) shall—

(a) be measures other than the provision of personal protective equipment or of information, instruction, training and supervision, so far as is reasonably practicable; and

(b) include, where appropriate, measures to minimise the effects of the hazard as well as to reduce the likelihood of the hazard occurring.

(3) The hazards referred to in paragraph (1) are—

(a) any article or substance falling or being ejected from work equipment;

(b) rupture or disintegration of parts of work equipment;

(c) work equipment catching fire or overheating;

(d) the unintended or premature discharge of any article or of any gas, dust, liquid, vapour or other substance which, in each case, is produced, used or stored in the work equipment;

(e) the unintended or premature explosion of the work equipment or any article or substance produced, used or stored in it.

(4) For the purposes of this regulation "adequately" means adequately having regard only to the nature of the hazard and the nature and degree of exposure to the risk.

(5) This regulation shall not apply where any of the following Regulations apply in respect of any risk to a person's health or safety for which such Regulations require measures to be taken to prevent or control such risk, namely—

(a) the Ionising Radiations Regulations 1985(1);

(b) the Control of Asbestos at Work Regulations 1987(2);

(c) the Control of Substances Hazardous to Health Regulations 1994(3);

(d) the Noise at Work Regulations 1989(4);

(e) the Construction (Head Protection) Regulations 1989(5);

(f) the Control of Lead at Work Regulations 1998(6).

Controls for starting or making a significant change in operating conditions

14.—(1) Every employer shall ensure that, where appropriate, work equipment is provided with one or more controls for the purposes of—

(a) starting the work equipment (including re-starting after a stoppage for any reason); or

(b) controlling any change in the speed, pressure or other operating conditions of the work equipment where such conditions after the change result in risk to health and safety which is greater than or of a different nature from such risks before the change.

(2) Subject to paragraph (3), every employer shall ensure that, where a control is required by paragraph (1), it shall not be possible to perform any operation mentioned in sub-paragraph (a) or (b) of that paragraph except by a deliberate action on such control.

(3) Paragraph (1) shall not apply to re-starting or changing operating conditions as a result of the normal operating cycle of an automatic device.

Stop controls

15.—(1) Every employer shall ensure that, where appropriate, work equipment is provided with one or more readily accessible controls the operation of which will bring the work equipment to a safe condition in a safe manner.

(2) Any control required by paragraph (1) shall bring the work equipment to a complete stop where necessary for reasons of health and safety.

(3) Any control required by paragraph (1) shall, if necessary for reasons of health and safety, switch off all sources of energy after stopping the functioning of the work equipment.

(4) Any control required by paragraph (1) shall operate in priority to any control which starts or changes the operating conditions of the work equipment

Emergency stop controls

16.—(1) Every employer shall ensure that, where appropriate, work equipment is provided with one or more readily accessible emergency stop controls unless it is not necessary by reason of the nature of the hazards and the time taken for the work equipment to come to a complete stop as a result of the action of any control provided by virtue of regulation 15(1).

(2) Any control required by paragraph (1) shall operate in priority to any control required by regulation 15(1).

Controls

17.—(1) Every employer shall ensure that all controls for work equipment are clearly visible and identifiable, including by appropriate marking where necessary.

(2) Except where necessary, the employer shall ensure that no control for work equipment is in a position where any person operating the control is exposed to a risk to his health or safety.

(3) Every employer shall ensure where appropriate—

(a) that, so far as is reasonably practicable, the operator of any control is able to ensure from the position of that control that no person is in a place where he would be exposed to any risk to his health or safety as a result of the operation of that control, but where or to the extent that it is not reasonably practicable;

(b) that, so far as is reasonably practicable, systems of work are effective to ensure that, when work equipment is about to start, no person is in a place where he would be exposed to a risk to his health or safety as a result of the work equipment starting, but where neither of these is reasonably practicable;

(c) that an audible, visible or other suitable warning is given by virtue of regulation 24 whenever work equipment is about to start.

(4) Every employer shall take appropriate measures to ensure that any person who is in a place where he would be exposed to a risk to his health or safety as a result of the starting or stopping of work equipment has sufficient time and suitable means to avoid that risk.

Stability

20. Every employer shall ensure that work equipment or any part of work equipment is stabilised by clamping or otherwise where necessary for purposes of health or safety.

Lighting

21. Every employer shall ensure that suitable and sufficient lighting, which takes account of the operations to be carried out, is provided at any place where a person uses work equipment.

Maintenance operations
22. Every employer shall take appropriate measures to ensure that work equipment is so constructed or adapted that, so far as is reasonably practicable, maintenance operations which involve a risk to health or safety can be carried out while the work equipment is shut down, or in other cases—
(a) maintenance operations can be carried out without exposing the person carrying them out to a risk to his health or safety; or
(b) appropriate measures can be taken for the protection of any person carrying out maintenance operations which involve a risk to his health or safety.

Markings
23. Every employer shall ensure that work equipment is marked in a clearly visible manner with any marking appropriate for reasons of health and safety

Warnings
24.—(1) Every employer shall ensure that work equipment incorporates any warnings or warning devices which are appropriate for reasons of health and safety.
(2) Without prejudice to the generality of paragraph (1), warnings given by warning devices on work equipment shall not be appropriate unless they are unambiguous, easily perceived and easily understood.

Employees carried on mobile work equipment
25. Every employer shall ensure that no employee is carried by mobile work equipment unless—
(a) it is suitable for carrying persons; and
(b) it incorporates features for reducing to as low as is reasonably practicable risks to their safety, including risks from wheels or tracks.

Interpretation

The HSE guidance on Health and Safety at Work, which can be found at http://www.hse.gov.uk/pubns/indg291.pdf provides some useful guidance in relation to the interpretation of the Regulations as follows. These are a good port of call when considering pleadings:-

A combination of these measures may be necessary depending on the requirements of the work, your assessment of the risks involved, and the practicability of such measures.

Machinery

Why is machinery safety important?
Working with machinery can be dangerous because moving machinery can cause injuries in many ways:

- *People can be hit and injured by moving parts of machinery or ejected material. Parts of the body can also be drawn into or trapped between rollers, belts and pulley drives.*

- *Sharp edges can cause cuts and severing injuries, sharp-pointed parts can stab or puncture the skin, and rough surface parts can cause friction or abrasion.*

- *People can be crushed both between parts moving together or towards a fixed part of the machine, wall or other object, and two parts moving past one another can cause shearing.*

- *Parts of the machine, materials and emissions (such as steam or water) can be hot or cold enough to cause burns or scalds and electricity can cause electrical shock and burns.*

- *Injuries can also occur due to machinery becoming unreliable and developing faults due to poor or no maintenance or when machines are used improperly through inexperience or lack of training.*

Before you start

Before allowing someone to start using any machine you need to think about what risks there are and how these can be managed. You should:

- *Check that it is complete, with all safeguards fitted, and free from defects. The term 'safeguard' includes guards, interlocks, two-hand controls, light guards, pressure-sensitive mats etc. By law, the sup-*

plier must provide the right safeguards and inform buyers of any risks ('residual risks') that users need to be aware of and manage because they could not be designed out.

- *Produce a safe system of work for using and maintaining the machine. Maintenance may require the inspection of critical features where deterioration would cause a risk. Also look at the residual risks identified by the manufacturer in the information/instructions provided with the machine and make sure they are included in the safe system of work.*

- *Ensure every static machine has been installed properly and is stable (usually fixed down) and is not in a location where other workers, customers or visitors may be exposed to risk.*

- *Choose the right machine for the job. Note that new machines should be CE marked and be supplied with a Declaration of Conformity and instructions in English.*

Make sure the machine is:

- *safe for any work that has to be done when setting up, during normal use, when clearing blockages, when carrying out repairs for breakdowns, and during planned maintenance;*

- *properly switched off, isolated or locked-off before taking any action to remove blockages, clean or adjust the machine.*

Also, make sure you identify and deal with the risks from:

- *electrical, hydraulic or pneumatic power supplies;*

- *badly designed safeguards. These may be inconvenient to use or easily overridden, which could encourage your workers to risk injury and break the law. If they are, find out why they are doing it and take appropriate action to deal with the reasons/causes.*

Preventing access to dangerous parts

Think about how you can make a machine safe. The measures you use to prevent access to dangerous parts should be in the following order. In some cases it may be necessary to use a combination of these measures:

- *Use fixed guards (eg secured with screws or nuts and bolts) to enclose the dangerous parts, whenever practicable. Use the best material for these guards – plastic may be easy to see through but may easily be damaged. Where you use wire mesh or similar materials, make sure the holes are not large enough to allow access to moving parts.*

- *If fixed guards are not practicable, use other methods, eg interlock the guard so that the machine cannot start before the guard is closed and cannot be opened while the machine is still moving. In some cases, trip systems such as photoelectric devices, pressure-sensitive mats or automatic guards may be used if other guards are not practicable.*

- *Where guards cannot give full protection, use jigs, holders, push sticks etc if it is practicable to do so.*

- *Control any remaining risk by providing the operator with the necessary information, instruction, training, supervision and appropriate safety equipment.*

Other things you should consider

- *Adequate training should ensure that those who use the machine are competent to use it safely. This includes ensuring they have the correct skills, knowledge, experience and risk awareness, and are physically suited to the task. Sometimes formal qualifications are needed, eg for chainsaw operators.*

- *Ensure control switches are clearly marked to show what they do.*

- *Have emergency stop controls where necessary, eg mushroom-head push buttons within easy reach.*

- *Make sure operating controls are designed and placed to avoid accidental operation and injury, use two-hand controls where necessary and shroud start buttons and pedals.*

- *Do not let un-authorised, unqualified or untrained people use machinery – never allow children to operate or help at machines. Some workers, eg new starters, young people or those with disabilities, may be particularly at risk and need instruction, training and supervision.*

- *If machines are controlled by programmable electronic systems, changes to any programmes should be carried out by a competent person (someone who has the necessary skills, knowledge and experience to carry out the work safely). Keep a record of such changes and check they have been made properly.*
- *Ensure the work area around the machine is kept clean and tidy, free from obstructions or slips and trips hazards, and well lit.*

Mobile work equipment

In addition to these general requirements which apply to all work equipment, Part III of PUWER contains specific duties regarding mobile work equipment, for example fork-lift trucks and dumper trucks.

You should ensure that where mobile work equipment is used for carrying people, it is suitable for this purpose. Measures should be taken to reduce the risks (eg from it rolling over) to the safety of the people being carried, the operator and anyone else.

Power presses

Part IV of the Regulations also contains specific requirements regarding power presses. In particular, you should have a power press, and associated guard or protection device, thoroughly examined at specified intervals and inspected daily when it is in use to ensure that it is safe. This work should only be performed by a competent person and records should be kept.

Dos and don'ts of machinery safety

As the dutyholder you should ensure that all employees likely to use machinery understand and follow these dos and don'ts:
Do...

- ✔ *check the machine is well maintained and fit to be used, ie appropriate for the job, working properly and all the safety measures are in place – guards, isolators, locking mechanisms, emergency off switches etc;*
- ✔ *use the machine properly and in accordance with the manufacturer's instructions;*

✔ *make sure employees are wearing the appropriate protective clothing and equipment, required for that machine, such as safety glasses, hearing protection and safety shoes;*

✔ *ensure that those who use machinery are competent to use it safely, provide training where necessary. For some machinery a formal qualification is needed.*

Don't...

✗ *use a machine or appliance that has a danger sign or tag attached to it. Danger signs should only be removed by an authorised person who is satisfied that the machine or process is now safe;*

✗ *remove any safeguards, even if their presence seems to make the job more difficult;*

✗ *wear dangling chains, loose clothing, rings or have loose long hair that could get caught up in moving parts;*

✗ *distract people who are using machines.*

Plant and equipment maintenance
Why is maintenance of plant and equipment important?

Additional hazards can occur when plant and equipment becomes unreliable and develops faults. Maintenance allows these faults to be diagnosed early, to manage any risks. However, maintenance needs to be correctly planned and carried out. Unsafe maintenance has caused many fatalities and serious injuries either during the maintenance or to those using badly maintained or wrongly maintained/repaired equipment.

An effective maintenance programme will make plant and equipment more reliable. Fewer breakdowns will mean less dangerous contact with machinery is required, as well as having the cost benefits of better productivity and efficiency.

The Provision and Use of Work Equipment Regulations 1998 require work equipment and plant to be maintained so that it remains safe and that the maintenance operation is carried out safely.

What do I have to do?

If you are an employer and you provide equipment for use (such as hammers, knives and ladders or electrical power tools and larger plant), you need to demonstrate that you have arrangements in place to make sure it is maintained in a safe condition.

Think about what hazards can occur:

- *if tools break during use;*

- *if machinery starts up unexpectedly;*

- *if there is contact with materials that are normally enclosed within the machine, ie caused by leaks/breakage/ejection etc*

Failing to correctly plan and communicate clear instructions and information before starting maintenance can lead to confusion and can cause accidents. This can be a particular problem if maintenance is carried out during normal production work or where there are contractors who are unfamiliar with the site.

Extra care is also required if maintenance involves:

- *working at height or doing work that requires access to unusual parts of the building;*

- *entering vessels or confined spaces where there may be toxic materials or a lack breathable of air.*

How can I do it?

Establishing a planned maintenance programme may be a useful step towards reducing risk, as well as having a reporting procedure for workers who may notice problems while working on machinery.

Some items of plant and equipment may have safety-critical features where deterioration would cause a risk. You must have arrangements in place to make sure the necessary inspections take place.

But there are other steps to consider:

Before you start maintenance

- *Decide if the work should be done by specialist contractors. Never take on work for which you are not competent or not prepared.*

- *Plan the work carefully before you start, ideally using the manufacturer's maintenance instructions, and produce a safe system of work. This will reduce the risks and avoid unforeseen delays.*
- *Make sure maintenance staff are competent and have appropriate clothing and equipment.*
- *Try and use downtime for maintenance. You can avoid the difficulties in coordinating maintenance and lost production if maintenance work is performed before start-up or during shutdown periods.*

Safe working areas
- *You must provide safe access and a safe place of work.*
- *Don't just focus on the safety of maintenance workers – take the necessary precautions to ensure the safety of others who may be affected by their work, eg other employees or contractors working nearby.*
- *Set up signs and barriers and position people at key points if they are needed to keep other people out.*

Plant and equipment must be made safe before maintenance starts. Safe isolation
- *Ensure moving plant has stopped and that it is isolated from electrical and other power supplies. Most maintenance should be carried out with the power off. If the work is near uninsulated, overhead electrical conductors, eg close to overhead travelling cranes, cut the power off to these first.*
- *Lock off machines if there is a chance the power could be accidentally switched back on.*
- *Isolate plant and pipelines containing pressured fluid, gas, steam or hazardous material. Lock off isolating valves.*

Other factors you need to consider
- *Release any stored energy, such as compressed air or hydraulic pressure that could cause the machine to move or cycle.*

- *Support parts of plant that could fall, eg support the blades of down-stroking bale cutters and guillotines with blocks.*
- *Allow components that operate at high temperatures time to cool.*
- *Place mobile plant in neutral gear, apply the brake and chock the wheels.*
- *Safely clean out vessels containing flammable solids, liquids, gases or dusts,*
- *and check them before hot work is carried out, to prevent explosions. You may need specialist help and advice to do this safely.*
- *Avoid entering tanks, vessels or confined spaces where possible. These spaces can have additional hazards due to the atmosphere or risks of fire etc. If required, get specialist help to ensure adequate precautions are taken.*
- *Clean and check vessels containing toxic materials before work starts. If*
- *required, get specialist help to ensure adequate precautions are taken.*
- *Ensure that those who are doing the maintenance are competent to carry out*
- *the work. You may need to provide training to ensure that competence.*

Do...

- ✔ *ensure maintenance is carried out by a competent person (someone who has the necessary skills, knowledge and experience to carry out the work safely);*
- ✔ *maintain plant and equipment regularly – use the manufacturer's maintenance instructions as a guide, particularly if there are safety-critical features;*
- ✔ *have a procedure that allows workers to report damaged or faulty equipment;*
- ✔ *provide the proper tools for the maintenance person;*
- ✔ *schedule maintenance to minimise the risk to other workers and the maintenance person wherever possible;*

✔ *make sure maintenance is done safely, that machines and moving parts are isolated or locked and that flammable/explosive/toxic materials are dealt with properly.*

Don't...

✗ *ignore maintenance;*

✗ *ignore reports of damaged or unsafe equipment;*

✗ *use faulty or damaged equipment.*

Investigating Work Equipment Regulations Cases Post ERRA

It is always worth remembering that for Post ERR Act cases, the Claimant Lawyer will need to prove negligence. Some key points to consider are:-

1. If there is a defect with the work equipment, can you prove what this was? It may be worth considering expert evidence for more complex work equipment.

2. Can you show lack of maintenance or inspection of the work equipment was the cause of the accident? Again expert evidence may be required.

3. Consider obtaining disclosure of maintenance and inspection records, but consider this may only be relevant if it can be shown lack of maintenance of inspection was the cause of the accident.

4. Some cases may relate to guards or other safety features of work equipment. It is always worth considering contacting the manufacturers of the work equipment to consider what safety features should have been in place.

5. Training records in work equipment cases are helpful to obtain, if the cause of the accident was lack of training, but one must again consider evidence as to what training should have been

provided and how the lack of training was causative of the accident.

6. Even though the 1998 Regulations no longer impose strict liability, it is still useful to plead the relevant Regulations for post ERRA cases, as they are a useful guide as to the likely standards of care.

Another Example

AILEEN COOPER v BRIGHT HORIZONS FAMILY SOLUTIONS LTD (2013), found that the Defendant was in breach of PUWER in failing to maintain a cot in an efficient state and working order. The facts of the case are referred to in chapter 9. The Judgment sets out:-

42. *I am satisfied that there was a breach of the absolute obligation contained in Regulation 5(1) of the Provision and Use of Work Equipment Regulations 1998 to maintain the cot in in an efficient state, in efficient working order and in good repair, and in so far as it is necessary, for the reasons set out below, there were also breaches of Regulations 8 and 9. In my view the injury was caused by the inability of Mrs Cooper to put the side down. If she had been able to do, she would have been able to bend her knees and put the baby down without exerting any, or any substantial, force on her back.*

43. *In Ball v Street [2004] EWCA Civ 76 Potter LJ considered Stark v The Post Office [2000] ICR 1013, CA in which it was held that an absolute obligation was imposed by the corresponding previous regulation, namely Regulation 6(1) of the Provision and Use of Work Equipment Regulations 1992.*

44. *Potter LJ said at paras 38 and 39:*

"38. *The employer's duty of care laid down by Regulation 5(1) applies to any work equipment 'used at work': see Regulation 3. As the judge held, and I have already confirmed, the Defendant was within Regulation 3 in relation to the maintenance of the haybob and was subject to the employer's duty to see that it was "maintained in an efficient state, in efficient working order and in good repair".*

39. That was a duty in similar terms to the duty imposed by sections 22(1) and 152(1) of the Factories Act 1937, and alleged to have been breached in respect of the failed hoist mechanism in Galashiels v Millar. The headnote to the report of the House of Lords' decision in that case accurately sets out the ratio of the decision, namely that the duty imposed an absolute and continuing obligation, so that proof of any failure in the mechanism of a hoist or lift established a breach of statutory duty, even though it was impossible to anticipate such failure before the event or to explain it afterwards, and even though all reasonable steps had been taken to provide a suitable hoist or lift and to maintain it properly."

45. He said at para 44:

*"In relation to Regulation 5(1), I do not accept the broad proposition of the judge that, where there is an expendable part in a machine known to break from time to time which can easily be replaced and it is one of a number of such parts so that the mechanism can continue working in an overall effective and efficient manner, no breach of Regulation 5(1) is demonstrable, "just like when one light bulb goes in a chandelier containing a large number of electric light bulbs." The Regulation does not define the employer's duty in terms of the overall suitability of the equipment to perform the task for which it is designed. **It deals with the duty to maintain it in an efficient state and working order and in good repair in respect of all of its mechanical parts so as to prevent injury to the person using the** equipment. As in the case of the sections of the Factories Act 1937 considered in Galashiels v Millar, the object of the Regulations is a broad one, **namely to protect workmen, and the task of the court is to view the maintenance and the condition of the machinery sup-***

plied to them from the point of view of health and safety and not that of productivity or economy."

46. *In my view the cot was not in an efficient state or in efficient working order or in good repair. I am satisfied that the mechanism for putting the cot side down was broken. I reject the submission that the cot side was held up in a fixed position by cable ties solely to stop the side being put down to prevent babies falling from the cot. Mrs Cooper and Ms Richmond's evidence is that the fact that the mechanism for operating the sides of the cot was broken had been reported to Ms Macer and they were aware that other staff had also done so.*

47. *I am satisfied that the cot was defective notwithstanding that other cots were available with sides that could not be put down. There is no material before me about the particular construction of the cots, with or without sides capable of being put down, or the height of the sides or distance of the base of the cots from the floor. There is no information about the allocation of cots or whether babies of different ages and weights were put into different types of cots. **The plain fact, however, is that a cot which was designed to have the side put down could not be put down because the mechanism was broken.***

Points to Note

1. The Court will likely look at PUWER cases from the perspective of health and safety i.e. As in the case of the sections of the *Factories Act 1937* considered in **Galashiels v Millar,** *the object of the Regulations is a broad one,* **namely to protect workmen, and the task of the court is to view the maintenance and the condition of the machinery supplied to them from the point of view of health and safety and not that of productivity or economy.".** The Court will examine the maintenance and condition of the work equipment and therefore disclosure of records will be important.

2. In the above case the *'mechanism was broken'.* In order to succeed under PUWER, the Claimant will need to identify the exact defect and how this was causative of the accident, especially for post ERRA cases, where common law negligence will have to be proved, in other words that the defect would have been reasonably foreseeable through either lack of maintenance or inspection.

Conclusions

Old work equipment cases were arguably fairly straightforward in terms of strict liability. Most cases at the time of writing this text are likely to involve proving negligence in such cases. It is important to consider the 1998 Regulations in detail when drafting pleadings, some of which are very fact specific and consider closely whether lack of training, maintenance or inspection etc. contributed to the accident and if so how?

CHAPTER ELEVEN
THE PERSONAL PROTECTIVE EQUIPMENT REGULATIONS 1992 AND THE MANAGEMENT OF HEALTH & SAFETY REGULATIONS 1999

This chapter seeks to set out and look at two important sets of Regulations that may apply to a number of workplace scenarios.

The PPE Regulations 1992

The Regulations set out as follows:-

Provision of personal protective equipment

4.—(1) Every employer shall ensure that suitable personal protective equipment is provided to his employees who may be exposed to a risk to their health or safety while at work except where and to the extent that such risk has been adequately controlled by other means which are equally or more effective.

(2) Every self-employed person shall ensure that he is provided with suitable personal protective equipment where he may be exposed to a risk to his health or safety while at work except where and to the extent that such risk has been adequately controlled by other means which are equally or more effective.

(3) Without prejudice to the generality of paragraphs (1) and (2), personal protective equipment shall not be suitable unless—

(a) it is appropriate for the risk or risks involved and the conditions at the place where exposure to the risk may occur;
(b) it takes account of ergonomic requirements and the state of health of the person or persons who may wear it;

(c) it is capable of fitting the wearer correctly, if necessary, after adjustments within the range for which it is designed;

(d) so far as is practicable, it is effective to prevent or adequately control the risk or risks involved without increasing overall risk;

(e) it complies with any enactment (whether in an Act or instrument) which implements in Great Britain any provision on design or manufacture with respect to health or safety in any relevant Community directive listed in Schedule 1 which is applicable to that item of personal protective equipment.

Compatibility of personal protective equipment

5.—(1) Every employer shall ensure that where the presence of more than one risk to health or safety makes it necessary for his employee to wear or use simultaneously more than one item of personal protective equipment, such equipment is compatible and continues to be effective against the risk or risks in question.

(2) Every self-employed person shall ensure that where the presence of more than one risk to health or safety makes it necessary for him to wear or use simultaneously more than one item of personal protective equipment, such equipment is compatible and continues to be effective against the risk or risks in question.

Assessment of personal protective equipment

6.—(1) Before choosing any personal protective equipment which by virtue of regulation 4 he is required to ensure is provided, an employer or self-employed person shall ensure that an assessment is made to determine whether the personal protective equipment he intends will be provided is suitable.

(2) The assessment required by paragraph (1) shall include—

(a) an assessment of any risk or risks to health or safety which have not been avoided by other means;

(b) the definition of the characteristics which personal protective equipment must have in order to be effective against the risks referred to in sub-paragraph (a) of this paragraph, taking into account any risks which the equipment itself may create;

(c) comparison of the characteristics of the personal protective equipment available with the characteristics referred to in sub-paragraph (b) of this paragraph.

(3) Every employer or self-employed person who is required by paragraph (1) to ensure that any assessment is made shall ensure that any such assessment is reviewed if—

(a) there is reason to suspect that it is no longer valid; or

(b) there has been a significant change in the matters to which it relates,

and where as a result of any such review changes in the assessment are required, the relevant employer or self-employed person shall ensure that they are made.

Maintenance and replacement of personal protective equipment

7.—(1) Every employer shall ensure that any personal protective equipment provided to his employees is maintained (including replaced or cleaned as appropriate) in an efficient state, in efficient working order and in good repair.

(2) Every self-employed person shall ensure that any personal protective equipment provided to him is maintained (including replaced or cleaned as appropriate) in an efficient state, in efficient working order and in good repair.

Information, instruction and training

9.—(1) Where an employer is required to ensure that personal protective equipment is provided to an employee, the employer shall also ensure that the employee is provided with such information, instruction and training as is adequate and appropriate to enable the employee to know—

(a) the risk or risks which the personal protective equipment will avoid or limit;

(b) the purpose for which and the manner in which personal protective equipment is to be used; and

(c) any action to be taken by the employee to ensure that the personal protective equipment remains in an efficient state, in efficient working order and in good repair as required by regulation 7(1).

(2) Without prejudice to the generality of paragraph (1), the inform-ation and instruction provided by virtue of that paragraph shall not be adequate and appropriate unless it is comprehensible to the persons to whom it is provided.

Use of personal protective equipment

10.—*(1) Every employer shall take all reasonable steps to ensure that any personal protective equipment provided to his employees by virtue of regulation 4(1) is properly used.*

(2) Every employee shall use any personal protective equipment provided to him by virtue of these Regulations in accordance both with any training in the use of the personal protective equipment concerned which has been received by him and the instructions respecting that use which have been provided to him by virtue of regulation 9.

(3) Every self-employed person shall make full and proper use of any personal protective equipment provided to him by virtue of regulation 4(2).

(4) Every employee and self-employed person who has been provided with personal protective equipment by virtue of regulation 4 shall take all reasonable steps to ensure that it is returned to the accommodation provided for it after use.

Points to Note

1. The Regulations post ERRA are not binding as to breach of duty, but may be a guide as to the duty of an employer.

2. PPE cases will often feature in relation to cases where an employee has been working with sharp objects/materials, such as on a construction site.

3. The PPE Regulations will rarely be used on their own and are more often combined with other relevant regulations.

4. The fact there was no risk assessment will not automatically mean the Defendant is in breach of duty, the lack of a risk assessment must be shown to be a cause of the accident.

5. Always consider all the relevant risk assessment Regulations when considering your cases such as:-

    a) Risk assessment - had the defendant undertaken one, and if so did it deal with the risk? If the risk had been identified and the risk assessment has been breached, it may be an indictor the defendant is in breach of the common law duty of care?

    b) Training - had the claimant received adequate health and safety training and if not, why not? If there is a lack of training, this may indicate breach of the common law duty of care.

    c) Instructions - was the claimant instructed in how to undertake a particular task safely, especially if it involves dangerous equipment or scenarios with a risk to health and safety. Lack of instructions could indicate a breach of the common law duty of care.

6. Health and safety policy - ask to see a copy of the employer's health and safety policy. Lack of a policy or person responsible for health and safety, may indicate a breach of duty.

7. In order to succeed, one must always consider how a lack of risk assessment, training, instructions etc. was causative of the accident. If for example, the accident scenario is so unusual that no risk assessment would reasonably identified such a risk, then a lack of a risk assessment is unlikely to indicate a breach of the common law duty of care to ensure the employee was reasonably safe.

8. The 1999 Regulations will be pleaded in most Particulars of Claim and are probably the most commonly cited Regulations in respect of a workplace injury claim.

9. Remember that for post section 69 ERRA cases, the common law duty breaches of the duty of care, must also be specifically pleaded.

10. Always consider when pleading a case all the relevant Regulations concerning PPE such as:

    a)   Maintenance – if the equipment was provided, has it been maintained?

    b)   Training – was the Claimant trained to use the PPE equipment?

    c)   Risk assessment – had the PPE equipment been risk assessed?

    d)   Suitability – had the suitability of the PPE equipment been risk assessed?

    e)   Availability – was the equipment readily available and in a suitable condition?

    f)   Use – had the employer ensured that the work equipment was being properly utilised?

A Useful Case – PPE

The issue of PPE was explored in the case of **SHAUN NAREY v ICELAND FOODS LTD (2015)**. The Claimant, a sales assistant who had been injured after a crate of shopping he was carrying fell onto his foot, had not made out his claim for breach of statutory duty and negligence against his employer. Part of the claim arose out of a failure to provide suitable footwear (PPE).

The argument in the case as to PPE from the Judgment were as follows:-

30. The defendant says it had no duty under this regulation to provide protective footwear because the risk of injury was controlled, was too small and/or remote and that steel toe capped boots would not have been suitable. The defendant says it consequently had no duty to make an assessment under Regulation 6.

31. With reference to the Blair case, the claimant asks me to consider the guidance in paragraph 5 in particular taken from the case of Threlfall v Kingston upon Hull City Council [2011] JCR 209 paragraph 42 as set out. The claimant says the defendant has to assess what the risk is and argues that the risk is the likelihood of occurrence multiplied by the magnitude of consequence. Paragraph 42 says:

"The concept of preventing a risk is easy to understand. The precaution stops the injury from happening at all. Controlling a risk is a less certain concept. A risk can be controlled either by reducing the likelihood of an adverse event happening or by reducing the harmful effect of the adverse event when it happens.

34. In relation to manual handling training and protective footwear, the claimant says the Personal Protective Equipment at Work Regulations 1992 are relevant only if the risk is not controlled by other means that are equally or more effective. In this case the crate fell out of the claimant's grasp and was human error and the defendant could have reduced the likelihood of this accident occurring by providing protective footwear and that it is not fair for the defendant to run a system on the basis it is not going to happen, but if it does then there will be a fractured toe. **I was asked to take into account that the claimant had training and had complied with it, that a loss of grip per se is not a lack of training but from an unknown cause and on a balance of probabilities he should have been supplied with protective footwear"**

The Court concluded:-

41. On the claim there has been negligence at common law, I do not consider that on the evidence the defendant failed to design, institute or operate or insure the institution or operation of a safe system of work or that the defendant exposed the claimant to a fore-seeable risk of injury or that the defendant failed to take any or any adequate care for the safety of the claimant.

Some Useful Guidance Concerning PPE

The HSE publishes some useful guidance concerning the use of PPE in various workplace scenarios which is set out below:-

http://www.hse.gov.uk/toolbox/ppe.htm

Employers have duties concerning the provision and use of personal protective equipment (PPE) at work.

PPE is equipment that will protect the user against health or safety risks at work. It can include items such as safety helmets, gloves, eye protection, high-visibility clothing, safety footwear and safety harnesses. It also includes respiratory protective equipment (RPE).

Why is PPE important?
Making the workplace safe includes providing instructions, procedures, training and supervision to encourage people to work safely and responsibly.
Even where engineering controls and safe systems of work have been applied, some hazards might remain. These include injuries to:
 the lungs, eg from breathing in contaminated air
 the head and feet, eg from falling materials
 the eyes, eg from flying particles or splashes of corrosive liquids
 the skin, eg from contact with corrosive materials
 the body, eg from extremes of heat or cold
PPE is needed in these cases to reduce the risk.
What do I have to do?
 Only use PPE as a last resort

If PPE is still needed after implementing other controls (and there will be circumstances when it is, eg head protection on most construction sites), you must provide this for your employees free of charge

You must choose the equipment carefully (see selection details below) and ensure employees are trained to use it properly, and know how to detect and report any faults

Selection and use
You should ask yourself the following questions:

Who is exposed and to what?

How long are they exposed for?

How much are they exposed to?

When selecting and using PPE:

Choose products which are CE marked in accordance with the Personal Protective Equipment Regulations 2002 – suppliers can advise you

Choose equipment that suits the user – consider the size, fit and weight of the PPE. If the users help choose it, they will be more likely to use it

If more than one item of PPE is worn at the same time, make sure they can be used together, eg wearing safety glasses may disturb the seal of a respirator, causing air leaks

Instruct and train people how to use it, eg train people to remove gloves without contaminating their skin. Tell them why it is needed, when to use it and what its limitations are

Other advice on PPE

Never allow exemptions from wearing PPE for those jobs that 'only take a few minutes'

Check with your supplier on what PPE is appropriate – explain the job to them

If in doubt, seek further advice from a specialist adviser

Maintenance
PPE must be properly looked after and stored when not in use, eg in a dry, clean cupboard. If it is reusable it must be cleaned and kept in good condition.
Think about:

> *using the right replacement parts which match the original, eg respirator filters*
>
> *keeping replacement PPE available*
>
> *who is responsible for maintenance and how it is to be done*
>
> *having a supply of appropriate disposable suits which are useful for dirty jobs where laundry costs are high, eg for visitors who need protective clothing*

Employees must make proper use of PPE and report its loss or destruction or any fault in it.

Monitor and review

> *Check regularly that PPE is used. If it isn't, find out why not*
>
> *Safety signs can be a useful reminder that PPE should be worn*
>
> *Take note of any changes in equipment, materials and methods – you may need to update what you provide*

Types of PPE you can use
Eyes
Hazards
Chemical or metal splash, dust, projectiles, gas and vapour, radiation
Options
Safety spectacles, goggles, face screens, faceshields, visors
Note
Make sure the eye protection chosen has the right combination of impact/dust/splash/molten metal eye protection for the task and fits the user properly
Head and neck
Hazards
Impact from falling or flying objects, risk of head bumping, hair getting tangled in machinery, chemical drips or splash, climate or temperature
Options

Industrial safety helmets, bump caps, hairnets and firefighters' helmets
Note

> *Some safety helmets incorporate or can be fitted with specially-designed eye or hearing protection*
>
> *Don't forget neck protection, eg scarves for use during welding*
>
> *Replace head protection if it is damaged*

Ears
Hazards
Noise – a combination of sound level and duration of exposure, very high-level sounds are a hazard even with short duration
Options
Earplugs, earmuffs, semi-insert/canal caps
Note

> *Provide the right hearing protectors for the type of work, and make sure workers know how to fit them*
>
> *Choose protectors that reduce noise to an acceptable level, while allowing for safety and communication*

Hands and arms
Hazards
Abrasion, temperature extremes, cuts and punctures, impact, chemicals, electric shock, radiation, vibration, biological agents and prolonged immersion in water
Options
Gloves, gloves with a cuff, gauntlets and sleeving that covers part or all of the arm
Note

> *Avoid gloves when operating machines such as bench drills where the gloves might get caught*
>
> *Some materials are quickly penetrated by chemicals – take care in selection, see HSE's skin at work website*
>
> *Barrier creams are unreliable and are no substitute for proper PPE*
>
> *Wearing gloves for long periods can make the skin hot and sweaty, leading to skin problems. Using separate cotton inner gloves can help prevent this*

Feet and legs
Hazards

Wet, hot and cold conditions, electrostatic build-up, slipping, cuts and punctures, falling objects, heavy loads, metal and chemical splash, vehicles

Options

Safety boots and shoes with protective toecaps and penetration-resistant, mid-sole wellington boots and specific footwear, eg foundry boots and chainsaw boots

Note

> *Footwear can have a variety of sole patterns and materials to help prevent slips in different conditions, including oil- or chemical-resistant soles. It can also be anti-static, electrically conductive or thermally insulating*
>
> *Appropriate footwear should be selected for the risks identified*

Lungs

Hazards

> *Oxygen-deficient atmospheres, dusts, gases and vapours*

Options – respiratory protective equipment (RPE)

> *Some respirators rely on filtering contaminants from workplace air. These include simple filtering facepieces and respirators and power-assisted respirators*
>
> *Make sure it fits properly, eg for tight-fitting respirators (filtering facepieces, half and full masks)*
>
> *There are also types of breathing apparatus which give an independent supply of breathable air, eg fresh-air hose, compressed airline and self-contained breathing apparatus*

Note

> *The right type of respirator filter must be used as each is effective for only a limited range of substances*
>
> *Filters have only a limited life. Where there is a shortage of oxygen or any danger of losing consciousness due to exposure to high levels of harmful fumes, only use breathing apparatus – never use a filtering cartridge*
>
> *You will need to use breathing apparatus in a confined space or if there is a chance of an oxygen deficiency in the work area*

If you are using respiratory protective equipment, look at HSE's publication Respiratory protective equipment at work: A practical guide

Whole body

Hazards

Heat, chemical or metal splash, spray from pressure leaks or spray guns, contaminated dust, impact or penetration, excessive wear or entanglement of own clothing

Options

Conventional or disposable overalls, boiler suits, aprons, chemical suits

Note

    The choice of materials includes flame-retardant, anti-static, chain mail, chemically impermeable, and high-visibility

    Don't forget other protection, like safety harnesses or life jackets

Emergency equipment

Careful selection, maintenance and regular and realistic operator training is needed for equipment for use in emergencies, like compressed-air escape breathing apparatus, respirators and safety ropes or harnesses.

The Management of Health and Safety at Work Regulations 1999

The Regulations set out as follows:-

Risk assessment

3.—(1) Every employer shall make a suitable and sufficient assessment of—

(a) the risks to the health and safety of his employees to which they are exposed whilst they are at work; and

(b) the risks to the health and safety of persons not in his employment arising out of or in connection with the conduct by him of his undertaking,

for the purpose of identifying the measures he needs to take to comply with the requirements and prohibitions imposed upon him by or under the relevant statutory provisions and by Part II of the Fire Precautions (Workplace) Regulations 1997.

(2) Every self-employed person shall make a suitable and sufficient assessment of—

(a) the risks to his own health and safety to which he is exposed whilst he is at work; and

(b) the risks to the health and safety of persons not in his employment arising out of or in connection with the conduct by him of his undertaking,

for the purpose of identifying the measures he needs to take to comply with the requirements and prohibitions imposed upon him by or under the relevant statutory provisions.

(3) Any assessment such as is referred to in paragraph (1) or (2) shall be reviewed by the employer or self-employed person who made it if—

(a) there is reason to suspect that it is no longer valid; or

(b) there has been a significant change in the matters to which it relates; and where as a result of any such review changes to an assessment are required, the employer or self-employed person concerned shall make them.

(4) An employer shall not employ a young person unless he has, in relation to risks to the health and safety of young persons, made or reviewed an assessment in accordance with paragraphs (1) and (5).

(5) In making or reviewing the assessment, an employer who employs or is to employ a young person shall take particular account of—

(a) the inexperience, lack of awareness of risks and immaturity of young persons;

(b) the fitting-out and layout of the workplace and the workstation;

(c) the nature, degree and duration of exposure to physical, biological and chemical agents;

(d) the form, range, and use of work equipment and the way in which it is handled;

(e) the organisation of processes and activities;

(f) the extent of the health and safety training provided or to be provided to young persons; and

(g) risks from agents, processes and work listed in the Annex to Council Directive 94/33/EC(1) on the protection of young people at work.

(6) Where the employer employs five or more employees, he shall record

———

(a) the significant findings of the assessment; and

(b) any group of his employees identified by it as being especially at risk.

Health and safety arrangements

5.—(1) Every employer shall make and give effect to such arrangements as are appropriate, having regard to the nature of his activities and the size of his undertaking, for the effective planning, organisation, control, monitoring and review of the preventive and protective measures.

(2) Where the employer employs five or more employees, he shall record the arrangements referred to in paragraph (1).

Health surveillance

6. Every employer shall ensure that his employees are provided with such health surveillance as is appropriate having regard to the risks to their health and safety which are identified by the assessment.

Health and safety assistance

7.—(1) Every employer shall, subject to paragraphs (6) and (7), appoint one or more competent persons to assist him in undertaking the measures he needs to take to comply with the requirements and prohibitions imposed upon him by or under the relevant statutory provisions and by Part II of the Fire Precautions (Workplace) Regulations 1997.

(2) Where an employer appoints persons in accordance with paragraph (1), he shall make arrangements for ensuring adequate co-operation between them.

(3) The employer shall ensure that the number of persons appointed under paragraph (1), the time available for them to fulfil their functions and the means at their disposal are adequate having regard to the size of his undertaking, the risks to which his employees are exposed and the distribution of those risks throughout the undertaking.

(4) The employer shall ensure that—

(a) any person appointed by him in accordance with paragraph (1) who is not in his employment—

(i) is informed of the factors known by him to affect, or suspected by him of affecting, the health and safety of any other person who may be affected by the conduct of his undertaking, and

(ii) has access to the information referred to in regulation 10; and

(b) any person appointed by him in accordance with paragraph (1) is given such information about any person working in his undertaking who is—

(I) employed by him under a fixed-term contract of employment, or

(ii) employed in an employment business,

as is necessary to enable that person properly to carry out the function specified in that paragraph.

(5) A person shall be regarded as competent for the purposes of paragraphs (1) and (8) where he has sufficient training and experience or knowledge and other qualities to enable him properly to assist in undertaking the measures referred to in paragraph (1).

(6) Paragraph (1) shall not apply to a self-employed employer who is not in partnership with any other person where he has sufficient training and experience or knowledge and other qualities properly to undertake the measures referred to in that paragraph himself.

(7) Paragraph (1) shall not apply to individuals who are employers and who are together carrying on business in partnership where at least one of the individuals concerned has sufficient training and experience or knowledge and other qualities—

(a) properly to undertake the measures he needs to take to comply with the requirements and prohibitions imposed upon him by or under the relevant statutory provisions; and

(b) properly to assist his fellow partners in undertaking the measures they need to take to comply with the requirements and prohibitions imposed upon them by or under the relevant statutory provisions.

(8) Where there is a competent person in the employer's employment, that person shall be appointed for the purposes of paragraph (1) in preference to a competent person not in his employment.

Procedures for serious and imminent danger and for danger areas

8.—(1) Every employer shall—

(a) establish and where necessary give effect to appropriate procedures to be followed in the event of serious and imminent danger to persons at work in his undertaking;

(b) nominate a sufficient number of competent persons to implement those procedures in so far as they relate to the evacuation from premises of persons at work in his undertaking; and

(c) ensure that none of his employees has access to any area occupied by him to which it is necessary to restrict access on grounds of health and safety unless the employee concerned has received adequate health and safety instruction.

(2) Without prejudice to the generality of paragraph (1)(a), the procedures referred to in that sub-paragraph shall—

(a) so far as is practicable, require any persons at work who are exposed to serious and imminent danger to be informed of the nature of the hazard and of the steps taken or to be taken to protect them from it;

(b) enable the persons concerned (if necessary by taking appropriate steps in the absence of guidance or instruction and in the light of their knowledge and the technical means at their disposal) to stop work and immediately proceed to a place of safety in the event of their being exposed to serious, imminent and unavoidable danger; and

(c) save in exceptional cases for reasons duly substantiated (which cases and reasons shall be specified in those procedures), require the persons concerned to be prevented from resuming work in any situation where there is still a serious and imminent danger.

(3) A person shall be regarded as competent for the purposes of paragraph (1)(b) where he has sufficient training and experience or knowledge and other qualities to enable him properly to implement the evacuation procedures referred to in that sub-paragraph.

Information for employees

10.—(1) Every employer shall provide his employees with comprehensible and relevant information on—

(a) the risks to their health and safety identified by the assessment;

(b) the preventive and protective measures;

(c) the procedures referred to in regulation 8(1)(a) and the measures referred to in regulation 4(2)(a) of the Fire Precautions (Workplace) Regulations 1997;

(d) the identity of those persons nominated by him in accordance with regulation 8(1)(b) and regulation 4(2)(b) of the Fire Precautions (Workplace) Regulations 1997; and

(e) the risks notified to him in accordance with regulation 11(1)(c).

(2) Every employer shall, before employing a child, provide a parent of the child with comprehensible and relevant information on—

(a) the risks to his health and safety identified by the assessment;
(b) the preventive and protective measures; and
(c) the risks notified to him in accordance with regulation 11(1)(c).
(3) The reference in paragraph (2) to a parent of the child includes—
(a) in England and Wales, a person who has parental responsibility, within the meaning of section 3 of the Children Act 1989(1), for him; and
(b) in Scotland, a person who has parental rights, within the meaning of section 8 of the Law Reform (Parent and Child) (Scotland) Act 1986(2) for him.
(1)

Capabilities and training

13.—(1) Every employer shall, in entrusting tasks to his employees, take into account their capabilities as regards health and safety.
(2) Every employer shall ensure that his employees are provided with adequate health and safety training—
(a) on their being recruited into the employer's undertaking; and
(b) on their being exposed to new or increased risks because of—
(i) their being transferred or given a change of responsibilities within the employer's undertaking,
(ii) the introduction of new work equipment into or a change respecting work equipment already in use within the employer's undertaking,
(iii) the introduction of new technology into the employer's undertaking, or
(iv) the introduction of a new system of work into or a change respecting a system of work already in use within the employer's undertaking.
(3) The training referred to in paragraph (2) shall—
(a) be repeated periodically where appropriate;
(b) be adapted to take account of any new or changed risks to the health and safety of the employees concerned; and
(c) take place during working hours.

Employees' duties

14.—*(1) Every employee shall use any machinery, equipment, dangerous substance, transport equipment, means of production or safety device provided to him by his employer in accordance both with any training in the use of the equipment concerned which has been received by him and the instructions respecting that use which have been provided to him by the said employer in compliance with the requirements and prohibitions imposed upon that employer by or under the relevant statutory provisions.*

(2) Every employee shall inform his employer or any other employee of that employer with specific responsibility for the health and safety of his fellow employees—

(a) of any work situation which a person with the first-mentioned employee's training and instruction would reasonably consider represented a serious and immediate danger to health and safety; and

(b) of any matter which a person with the first-mentioned employee's training and instruction would reasonably consider represented a shortcoming in the employer's protection arrangements for health and safety, in so far as that situation or matter either affects the health and safety of that first mentioned employee or arises out of or in connection with his own activities at work, and has not previously been reported to his employer or to any other employee of that employer in accordance with this paragraph.

Risk Assessments, Training and Capability – Some Useful Cases

The following examples are a number of reported recent EL cases, where the Claimant was found to be entirely at fault for the accident, despite a lack of risk assessments and other matters the employer had failed to address:-

In **SPENCER VAUGHAN v MINISTRY OF DEFENCE (2015)** the Court found that the Ministry of Defence had not breached its duty of care qua employer to a marine who had suffered serious injuries after executing a shallow dive in the sea while off duty on a training week. The marine had known at the time of the accident that there was a risk of injury diving into shallow water, he had had a genuine and informed choice about entering the sea, he was not acting in the course of his employment, and he was not subject to any lack of capacity.

The Court facts were as follows:-

"The Claimant, Spencer Vaughan, is aged 27. When he was 21 he enlisted in the Royal Marines. After completion of his basic training in July 2009 he was awarded his green beret and posted to 45 Commando in Arbroath. On 18th January 2010 he and five other Royal Marines from his company flew to Gran Canaria in order to take part in a week's Adventure Training Exercise. The purpose of the exercise was to provide Mne Vaughan and his colleagues with the opportunity to crew a yacht in the course of off-shore sailing around the Canaries. The yacht was skippered by a very experienced Royal Marine sailing instructor, Corporal Justin Sanders, assisted by a Lance Corporal Quirk who was being trained to take on the role of a skipper. Corporal Sanders had sailed the boat in October and November 2009 from the UK to the Canaries and had engaged in weekly exercises with different groups of Marines after his arrival in the Canaries. The weekly exercises were due to continue until about April 2010. This scheme was something he had overseen and supervised bi- annually for about 10 years prior to 2009

The exercise involving Marine Vaughan proceeded without incident until the 23rd January 2010. That was the last day of the trip for Marine Vaughan and his colleagues. The day before there had been a full day's sailing from Tenerife. The day had ended with the boat reaching Puerto de Mogan in Gran Canaria, a substantial holiday resort with a large marina. On the 23rd January the boat had only about 6 miles to sail in order to return to the point at which the Marines were to be dropped off and the next group was to join the boat. Because there was little or no wind on the morning of the 23rd January, Corporal Sanders decided to postpone the departure from Puerto de Mogan. The plan was to wait until lunchtime in the hope that the wind would pick up. Apparently it is the common weather pattern in that part of the Canaries for the wind to gather strength later in the day. Corporal Sanders told the Marines that they were free to do what they wanted until about 1.30 p.m.

What Marine Vaughan and his five colleagues did was to go the beach area at Puerto de Mogan. The beach was a normal tourist pleasure beach with a boom across the bay around which the beach ran, the purpose of the boom being to keep out any boats, jetskis or other craft. The beach was manned by lifeguards. It was being used by holiday-makers including families. Whilst they were there, Marine Vaughan went into the sea from the beach. When he was about waist deep in the water he executed a shallow dive into the sea. In doing so he struck his head on something below the surface of the water. As a result he sustained a fracture of his cervical spine which has resulted in incomplete tetraplegia.

Marine Vaughan's case is that his injury was caused by the breach of duty of the Defendant, the Defendant having the same duty to him as would be owed to an employee by virtue of Section 2 of the Crown Proceedings Act 1947. I am required only to determine the issue of liability. That involves consideration of the following issues:

How it was that Marine Vaughan sustained his injury. The duty owed to Marine Vaughan in the particular circumstances of the accident.

• Whether there was a breach of such duty as was owed by the Defendant to Marine Vaughan.
• In the event of a breach of duty by the Defendant being causative of the accident, the extent to which (if at all) Marine Vaughan was contributory negligent.

The Court concluded as to breach of duty on two crucial issues a) no risk assessment could have identified the risk and, b) the accident was just 'one of those things' i.e. there was no breach of duty:-

In the context of the claim as put on behalf of Marine Vaughan there was significant criticism of the risk assessment of the training

exercise on which he was engaged. This was on the basis that only the risks involved in off shore sailing were assessed in any formal manner. The risks in relation to on shore activities were not assessed. The argument was that this was far too narrow a view of the expedition. <u>I do not consider that it is necessary to consider this issue at any length. Risk assessment could not conceivably form part of Corporal Sanders's duty of care in relation to the on shore activities of the Marines outside the course of their "employment"</u>. In any event the case as put in his closing submissions by Mr Rawlinson Q.C. was that a simple warning about the relevant risks would have been sufficient.

In view of my conclusions thus far, the issue of contributory negligence does not arise. Marine Keenan in his witness statement described the accident as "just one of those things" i.e. a pure accident with no fault involved. I consider that this is a reasonable description of the event. Marine Vaughan did something that he had done many times before. I infer that other people did the same on the beach in question on the 23rd January 2010. Marine Vaughan made what was a momentary and minor
misjudgement. It would be harsh to say that in doing so he was careless of his own safety".

A similar example arises in **GEORGE EDWARD SHARP V ELNAUGH & SONS LTD (2006)**. The facts were as follows:-

"This action the Claimant Mr. George Edward Sharp ('Mr. Sharp') claims damages against his former employers Elnaugh & Sons Limited ('Elnaugh') for personal injury which he sustained when he fell from a ladder in the course of his work as an electrician on 15 January 2003 at the Broomfield Methodist Church.

At the date of the accident Mr. Sharp was 63 years of age and had worked as an electrician for more than forty years. The Defendant company are a family business who have been electrical contractors since 1911. Mr. Sharp had carried out work for Elnaugh on a self-

employed basis from 1991, but in 1999 he became a full time employee of Elnaugh, and that was the position when the accident occurred.

4. Elnaugh had installed electrical heaters in Broomfield Methodist Church some years previously. Mr. Len Windsor was a member of the congregation and the Property Steward. On Sunday 12 January 2003 three of the heaters failed to work, so on the Monday Mr. Windsor telephoned Elnaugh to ask them to inspect and repair the heaters. A copy of the relevant page of the job book was produced by Mr. Elnaugh: it is dated 13.1.03 and states 'Mr. Windsor [address and phone number] Broomfield Methodist Church Re 3 overhead heaters not working'.

5. Mr. Sharp was sent to Broomfield Methodist Church by Elnaugh on Wednesday 15 January 2003. It was his third job of the day, and he went there about 1.00 pm. He had previously been working at Ongar: see his work sheet for that day. The system was that each electrician telephoned Elnaugh's office when they had finished their job and were given the next one to carry out. It depended on who next became free as to which electrician attended a job. All Mr. Sharp was told by Elnaugh was that three overhead heaters were not working: that was all Elnaugh's office knew themselves.

6. What happened next according to Mr. Sharp is described in his witness statement [124]
'When I attended I found that the heaters were some 15 feet above floor level of the Church and that to reach them would require a ladder. I had not been advised by my employers that a ladder was required. I carried a stepladder which is my own property, but which is only some 5 rungs high within the van I used to carry out my work for Elnaughs. Elnaughs knew that I carried a stepladder.

I have worked as an electrician for well over forty years. On arriving at the Church my standard method in approaching the job that was assigned to me was first of all to go to the trip box to check that that was in order and operational. I heard the contacts clunk when I switched on and off which indicated to me that the control box appeared to be working. The next aspect to check in accordance with my standard procedure was to check the appliance or appliances that were not working. The heaters were in the main Church. I did not have a ladder long enough to reach them and I borrowed one from the Church that was supplied by the caretaker. I ascended the ladder and was undoing a screw on one of the heaters to gain access to it when I felt the ladder slide down the wall. I came down with it and hit my head under my chin on a rung of the ladder. I was knocked out and when I came to I saw two of my teeth lying beside me. I tried to get up but my legs gave way. I picked up the teeth that I saw and put them in a hankie. I made contact with Elnaugh's office by my mobile telephone. I told them that I had had an accident and that I needed an ambulance.'

The Case dealt with in detail as to the issue of pleadings and how it must be shown the relevant breach was causative of the accident as follows, and is an excellent example of whether a Judge looked at numerous breaches of alleged statutory duty and dismissed them all as follows:-

"In the Particulars of Claim the legal basis of the Claimant's case is that the accident was caused by the negligence and/or breach of statutory duty of the Defendant [4-7]. I shall deal with each of these allegations in turn, starting with the alleged breaches of statutory duty. Mr. Crowley reminds me that these are matters of strict liability, and in closing submissions he said that the Defendant is in breach of all of the regulations as alleged, and that all of these breaches are causative of the Defendant's injuries. **I deal further with this subject below, but I make the general observation at this stage that it is not enough for the Claimant to prove that the Defendant was in breach of a specific statutory or common law duty: the Claimant must also prove that this breach of duty caused (wholly or in part) the injury to the Claimant which is the subject of the claim.**

Breach of statutory duty

43. Failing, in breach of regulation 13 of the Workplace (Health, Safety and Welfare) Regulations 1992 to take suitable and effective measures to prevent the Claimant falling a distance likely to cause personal injury.

The Defendant denies that these Regulations apply to the Claimant's work as the application of these regulations is excluded by Regulation 3(1)(b) thereof [Defence para. 2 at 68]. In my judgment the Defendants are correct in this assertion. Regulation 3(1) states that 'These Regulations apply to every workplace but shall not apply to...(b) a workplace where the only activity being undertaken is construction work within the meaning assigned to that phrase by regulation 2(1) of the Construction (Health, Safety and Welfare) Regulations 1996.....'

44. Regulation 2(1) of the 1996 Regulations provides as follows:

'construction work' means the carrying out of any building, civil engineering or engineering construction work and includes any of the f o l l o w i n g   – ....(e) the installation, commissioning, maintenance, repair...of electrical...or similar services which are normally fixed within or to a structure'
It is common ground between the parties that the Construction (Health, Safety and Welfare) Regulations 1996 and the Provision and Use of Work Equipment Regulations 1998 applied to the Claimant's work, and therefore the 1992 Regulations do not apply.

45. Failing, in breach of Regulation 5(1) of the Construction (Health, Safety and Welfare) Regulations 1996 to provide suitable and sufficient safe access to and egress from every place of work
Regulation 5(1) provides that
'There shall, so far as is reasonably practicable, be suitable and sufficient safe access to and egress from every place of work and to any other place provided for the use of any person while at work, which access shall be without risks to health and properly maintained'

46. The Defendant accepts that Broomfield Methodist Church was the Claimant's 'place of work' for the time that he was there, and that more particularly the location of the electrical heaters was also the Claimant's place of work.

*47. There had therefore to be a suitable and safe means of access and egress for the Claimant to and from the location of the electrical heaters. The Regulation does not however specify that the Employer himself must provide that suitable and safe means of access, but the Employer is in breach of his duty if a suitable and safe means of access does not exist. **I have found as a fact that the ladder provided by Mr. Windsor complied with this requirement and that Mr. Windsor was available to foot it, and therefore this breach is not made out.***

48. Failing, in breach of Regulation 5(2) of the Construction (Health, Safety and Welfare) Regulations 1996 to make and keep safe without risks to the health of the Claimant every place of work
Regulation 5(2) provides
'Every place of work shall, so far as is reasonably practicable, be made and kept safe for, and without risks to health to, any person at work there'

This is a general provision, and the manner in which it is alleged to have been breached I have already considered under Regulation 5(1) above. It is not alleged that the place of work was unsafe or contained other risks to health apart from the need to access the electrical heaters by ladder. This breach therefore is not made out by the Claimant.

49. Failing, in breach of Regulation 6(1) of the Construction (Health, Safety and Welfare) Regulations 1996, to take suitable and sufficient steps to prevent any person falling
Regulation 6(1), 6(5) and 6(6) provide
'(1) Suitable and sufficient steps shall be taken to prevent, so far as is reasonably practicable, any person falling
(5) A ladder shall not be used as, or as a means of access to or egress from, a place of work unless it is reasonable to do so having regard to –
(a) (b)
(a) (b)

50. sufficient means of access to the electric heaters: this is not a case where it is alleged that a scaffold tower was the only means of complying with this requirement, and in my judgment it was reasonable to use a ladder for the purpose of access, having regard to the nature of the work being carried out and its duration, which was not anticipated to be long, and the risks to the safety of Mr. Sharp in using the ladder, which were no greater than one would normally find.

51. In this context I have taken account of the fact that the top of the ladder was resting, not on the vertical wall of the building, but on the inward slope towards the ceiling, as the photographs show. I asked Mr. Sharp whether he considered this arrangement was less safe than placing the top of the ladder against a vertical wall, and he told me that the way in which he had placed the ladder was in fact more safe, since it was possible to some degree to wedge the top of the ladder against the slope. I accept this evidence from Mr. Sharp, who has a good deal of experience in placing and working from ladders.

52. In my judgement, the substance of the breach alleged under Regulation 6(1) is to be found in the alleged breaches of schedule 5, and for the reasons which follow I do not find a breach of Regulation 6(1) to be made out. I will take the next three allegations together.

53. Failing, in breach of Schedule 5 paragraphs 1, 2(b) and 2(c) of the Construction (Health, Safety and Welfare) Regulations 1996 to ensure that
(6) the nature of the work being carried out and its duration; and the risks to the safety of any person arising from the use of the ladder Where a ladder is used pursuant to paragraph (5) it shall comply with the provisions of Schedule 5; and the provisions of paragraph (3) shall not apply

50. Sufficient means of access to the electric heaters: this is not a case where it is alleged that a scaffold tower was the only means of complying with this requirement, and in my judgment it was reasonable to use a ladder for the purpose of access, having regard to the nature of the work being carried out and its duration, which was not anticipated to be long, and the risks to the safety of Mr. Sharp in using the ladder, which were no greater than one would normally find.

51. In this context I have taken account of the fact that the top of the ladder was resting, not on the vertical wall of the building, but on the inward slope towards the ceiling, as the photographs show. I asked Mr. Sharp whether he considered this arrangement was less safe than placing the top of the ladder against a vertical wall, and he told me that he way in which he had placed the ladder was in fact more safe, since it was possible to some degree to wedge the top of the ladder against the slope. I accept this evidence from Mr. Sharp, who has a good deal of experience in placing and working from ladders.

52. In my judgement, the substance of the breach alleged under Regulation 6(1) is to be found in the alleged breaches of schedule 5, and for the reasons which follow I do not find a breach of Regulation 6(1) to be made out. I will take the next three allegations together.

53. Failing, in breach of Schedule 5 paragraphs 1, 2(b) and 2(c) of the Construction (Health, Safety and Welfare) Regulations 1996 to ensure that

(6) the nature of the work being carried out and its duration; and the risks to the safety of any person arising from the use of the ladder

Where a ladder is used pursuant to paragraph (5) it shall comply with the provisions of Schedule 5; and the provisions of paragraph (3) shall not apply

The Claimant does not dispute that the use of a ladder was suitable and the surface on which the ladder was resting was stable, level and firm, and of sufficient strength and of suitable composition safely to support the ladder and any load intended to be placed on it (para. 1)

the ladder was erected so that it did not become displaced (para. 2(b))

the ladder was secured or footed (with a person positioned at the foot of the ladder) in order to prevent it slipping (para. 2(c))

54. Schedule 5 provides

1 Any surface upon which a ladder rests shall be stable, level and firm, of sufficient strength and of suitable composition safely to support the ladder and any load intended to be place upon it.

2 A ladder shall –

be suitable and of sufficient strength for the purposes or purposes for which it is being used be so erected as to ensure that it does not become displaced

where it is of a length when used of 3 metres or more, be secured to the extent that it is practicable to do so and where it is not practicable to secure the ladder a person shall be positioned at the foot of the ladder to prevent it slipping at all times when it is being used

(a)

(b) (c)

*55. a wood block floor. In itself I find that this floor was stable, level and firm, of sufficient strength and of suitable composition safely to support the ladder and the weight of Mr. Sharp upon it. There was an issue as to whether the surface of the floor had been polished so as to make it slippery and reduce the friction between its surface and the foot of the ladder, but **I accept Mr. Windsor's evidence that at the date of the accident the floor was cleaned regularly but not highly polished. I also find that the metal ladder which Mr. Windsor provided was suitable and of sufficient strength for the purpose for which it was being used: there is no suggestion that some defect in the ladder itself caused Mr. Sharp to fall.***

56. I have already found as a fact that the reason why Mr. Sharp fell from the ladder was because the ladder slipped, probably with the base slipping away from the wall. Paragraph 2(b) requires the ladder to be so erected as to ensure that it does not become displaced, as in fact occurred, but in my judgment there was nothing inherently unsafe about the way in which the ladder was placed. Neither Mr. Sharp nor Mr. Windsor had any concerns about the position of the ladder when Mr. Sharp first placed it in position and climbed up it to remove the screw holding the cover of the heater.

57. I find as a fact that the ladder in use was three metres or more in length, but it was not practicable to secure the ladder in the sense that in its location it could not be tied at the top or the bottom to a fixed structure. There was a possibility that a piece of furniture in the church could be moved to the foot of the ladder so that the ladder could rest against it, but in my view this was not practicable: it certainly did not occur to Mr. Sharp or Mr. Windsor to do this.

58. The case on liability really turns on the issue of whether the Defendants were at fault in failing to ensure that a person was placed at the foot of the ladder at all times while it was in use.

60. Failing, in breach of Regulation 4(1) of the Provision and Use of Work Equipment Regulations 1998 to ensure that the ladder was so constructed or adapted so as to be suitable for the purpose for which it was used or provided
Regulation 4(1) provides
'Every employer shall ensure that work equipment is so constructed or adapted as to be suitable for the purpose for which it is used or provided'
Although it is true that Elnaughs did not provide or inspect the ladder which was used by Mr. Sharp, there is no evidence that the ladder itself was not constructed or adapted so as to be suitable for the use to which it was put by Mr. Sharp: it is not alleged that the ladder was defective in any way. This breach is not established.

61. Failing, in breach of Regulation 4(2) of the Provision and Use of Work Equipment Regulations 1998 to have regard to the working conditions and risks which existed on the site where the ladder was required to be used and to have regard to the additional risks to the Claimant posed by the use of the ladder
Regulation 4(2) provides
'In selecting work equipment, every employer shall have regard to the working conditions and to the risks to the health and safety of persons which exist in the premises or undertaking in which that work equipment is to be used and any additional risk posed by the use of that work equipment'

62. Elnaughs did not in fact select the work equipment, but even assuming in the Claimant's favour that they had a duty to do so, there is no evidence that the site working conditions in themselves or the premises presented a risk to health and safety or that the use of the ladder posed any additional risk which affected health and safety. I have already noted that it was not the Claimant's case that some other type of work equipment should have been selected provided and used.

63. Failing, in breach of Regulation 4(3) of the Provision and Use of Work Equipment Regulations 1998 to ensure that a ladder was only used by the Claimant for operations and under conditions for which it was suitable
Regulation 4(3) provides
'Every employer shall ensure that work equipment is used only for operations for which, and under conditions for which, it is suitable.'
I find in this case that the ladder was being used for an operation for which it was suitable: as to the conditions under which it was being used, Mr. Windsor was available whenever necessary to foot the ladder. This breach is not substantiated

64. Failing, in breach of Regulation 8 of the Provision and Use of Work Equipment Regulations 1998, to ensure that the Claimant had adequate health and safety information and instructions available to him in respect of the use of ladders
Regulation 8 provides

'Every employer shall ensure that all persons who use work equipment have available to them adequate health and safety information and, where appropriate, written instructions pertaining to the use of the work equipment'

65. I have already dealt above with the health and safety inform-ation which was made available to Mr. Sharp by his employers, and while it is not the best presented I have seen, in my judgment it is adequate in its general terms, and specifically in respect of the use of ladders in working as an electrician. *A ladder is not a sophisticated piece of equipment, and Mr. Sharp had many years of experience in using long ladders at work. Nevertheless the modern law requires even experienced workman to be warned about the potential risks which arise from the use of standard equipment. There were in fact written instructions pertaining to the use of ladders provided by Elnaughs, and* *in my judgement they were adequate. Even if they were not, Mr. Sharp accepted that reading the health and safety policy would have made no difference.*

66. *Failing, in breach of Regulation 9 of the Provision and Use of Work Equipment Regulations 1998, to give the Claimant adequate training for the purposes of health and safety including training in the methods which may be adapted when using a ladder, any risks which its use may entail and precautions to be taken*
Regulation 9 provides
'Every employer shall ensure that all persons who use work equipment have received adequate training for purposes of health and safety, including training in the methods which may be adopted when using the work equipment, any risks which such use may entail and precautions to be taken.'

67. *These regulations embrace a wide variety of work equipment, some of which may be specialised tools or particularly dangerous to the uninitiated user.* **A long ladder however is a simple piece of equipment, and the risks in use are self-evident.** *The precautions to be taken when using a ladder at height are well known to any handyman, and Mr. Sharp had over forty years' experience working as an electrician.* **He accepted in evidence that he was well aware of the danger of a ladder moving while working at height and the need to have someone footing the ladder at all times.**

68. **It was accepted by Mr. Elnaugh that Mr. Sharp was not given any specific training in the use of ladders when he became an employee of Elnaugh in 1999, but Mr. Sharp had already been working for six years for Elnaugh on a self-employed basis, and the Company was entitled to take the view that Mr. Sharp was already a very experienced electrician who did not need training in such a basic matter.**

69. *Failing, in breach of Regulation 20 of the Provision and Use of Work Equipment Regulations 1998, to ensure that the ladder was stabilised*

Regulation 20 provides

'Every employer shall ensure that work equipment or any part of work equipment is stabilised by clamping or otherwise where necessary for purposes of health or safety'

70. The requirement to stabilise equipment in the case of a ladder can be achieved in a number of ways, as suggested by paragraph 2 of Schedule 5 to the 1996 Regulations cited above. Either it can be secured by being tied to a fixed point, or where it is not practicable to secure the ladder a person must be positioned at the foot of the ladder to prevent it slipping at all times when it is being used. There may be other means to stabilise a shorter ladder, such as the use of legs hinged at the top to form a step-ladder, but no specific alternatives were suggested on behalf of the Claimant. In my judgment it was sufficient to stabilise the ladder to ensure that someone was footing it at all times when in use. It was Mr. Sharp's decision to climb the ladder when he knew that Mr. Windsor was not there, and in my judgment breach of this Regulation is not made out"

The Judgment highlights numerous points made in this chapter as to how the alleged breach must be causative of the accident i.e

a) the Judgment here accepts there was a lack of training, but dismisses the point as the Claimant was an experienced employee, hence there is no breach of duty.

b) the Judgment accepted that there was no real health and safety training, but said *"A long ladder however is a simple piece of equipment, and the risks in use are self-evident".*

c) If an accident appears to be the claimant's own fault, consider very carefully how any alleged lack of training, risk assessments or health and safety policy contributed to the accident, especially if an employee had specific training or experience.

Indeed in this case the Court provided some very helpful guidance as to the issue of risk assessments:-

"It is undoubtedly good modern practice to undertake a risk assessment of any new job before starting work on it. The Claimant does not specifically refer to the Management of Health and Safety at Work Regulations 1999 but Regulation 3 provides that
'Every employer shall make a suitable and sufficient assessment of
(a) the risks to the health and safety of his employees to which they are exposed while they are at work.......
For the purpose of identifying the measures he needs to take to comply with the requirements and prohibitions imposed upon him by or under the relevant statutory provisions'

73. These Regulations are made under the Health and Safety at Work etc Act 1974, and under s.53 of the 1974 Act 'the relevant statutory provisions' means
1. (a) the provisions of this Part and of any health and safety regulations; and
2. (b) the existing statutory provisions
3.
The 'existing statutory provisions' are defined in s. 53 as the provisions in Schedule 1 of the 1974 Act, while and to the extent that they remain in force and any regulations made thereunder. The scope of 'the relevant statutory provisions' is therefore very wide. I note in the current edition of Redgrave's Health and Safety the following: at page 263:

'In Cross v Highlands and Islands Enterprises [2001] IRLR 336 OH the court rejected an argument that it was negligent in 1993 to fail to conduct a risk assessment as this regulation requires. It is not clear if the same result would apply to subsequent years, now that the duty is better known and more widely followed in practice (and contrast Bailey v Command Security Services & TJX Incorporated (25.10.01 unreported), QBD: negligent for employer not to conduct risk assessment.'

74. I am not however satisfied that these Regulations impose a strict civil liability upon an employer, which may well be the reason why counsel did not cite them to me. As noted by Redgrave at page 259:

'These Regulations were introduced in part under s. 15 of the HSWA 1974 and consequently provisions of that Act are relevant to the interpretation of the Regulations. A breach of the Regulations gives rise to potential criminal liability: see HWSA 1974 s. 33(1). In contrast to most of the other regulations introduced under the HSWA 1974, a breach of the Regulations does not give rise to civil liability with the exception of a breach of the duties in reg 16 or reg 19 (see reg 22). Although some commentators consider that the exclusion of civil liability amounted to defective implementation of the Framework Directive, such an argument was rejected in Cross v Highlands and Islands Enterprises.'

75. In my judgement therefore there is no strict civil liability upon an employer to carry out a risk assessment in the case of every job which an employee may undertake. <u>Having regard to modern business practice, it may be a breach of common law duty not to do so in some circumstances, but in my judgement the present matter is not such a case</u>. It must be reasonable for an employer to be able to take account of the knowledge and experience of his employees who have trade skills to make a preliminary assessment when visiting customers' premises of the likely requirements in respect of health and safety before work is carried out<u>. It would not be reasonable for example to send an apprentice to perform this task.</u> It is not a question of delegating the employer's responsibility: the question is whether the duty arises at all, and in my judgement here it does not".

The above however can be contrasted with the case of **STEPHEN P WHITESIDE v CROYDON LONDON BOROUGH COUNCIL (2010)**, where the lack of risk assessments was found to have contributed to the accident as follows. The facts from the Judgment were as follows:-

"Mr Whiteside suffered a work-related, stress-induced psychiatric injury in 1999 and, on his return to work, both he and LBC were advised by LBC's medical advisor that in order to control his stress levels so as to avoid a repetition of the breakdown he had suffered, he should avoid having to concentrate on multiple problems and work on single, specific tasks so as to avoid what was described as his organisational problems. Following his return to work throughout the return period from July 1999 until October 2004, he was provided with an excessive workload. This was coupled with poor management which failed to control or organise the workload of the professional staff working in the department he was appointed to, the Urban Design Department ("UDD"). The poor working conditions were exacerbated by a lack of any strategic guidance, support of the often contentious design work and advice that the UDD was asked to provide or interaction with the views and concerns being expressed to his line manager by Mr Whiteside in both formal annual job reviews and in less formal frequent contacts between them. **In addition, UDD never properly evaluated Mr Whiteside's job, never undertook any suitable or sufficient risk assessment of his susceptibility to work-related stress, never properly re-organised the management and supervision of the UDD despite an extended effort at doing so and never devised or implemented appropriate health and safety policies relating to stress- control and the reduction of the risk of stress-related psychiatric illness.** *Over the period that Mr Whiteside, who was already susceptible to stress-related health injures, was subjected to these problems, became more and more stressed. He drew these problems to the attention of LBC management, particularly in his job reviews, and his line managers ignored or failed to respond to these warnings and all the other obvious warning signs that Mr Whiteside was being subjected to unacceptable stress levels as a result of his working conditions. Following a particularly stressful period of working through 2004, Mr Whiteside's health completely broke down in October 2004. This breakdown was caused by the accumulation of the various factors already summarised.* **It was foreseeable that these factors gave rise to a significant increase in the risk of such a stress-related breakdown. These factors could and should have been avoided had LBC complied with its statutory duty of care in relation to Mr Whiteside in**

relation to his psychiatric health. In consequence, the resulting breakdown gives rise to a claim for damages for the psychiatric injury that he suffered.

LBC denies each step in Mr Whiteside's claim. It is therefore necessary to decide these issues: Did Mr Whiteside suffer a psychiatric injury?
If so, were Mr Whiteside's work and working conditions a substantial cause of that injury?
If so, was it foreseeable that these working conditions could cause Mr Whiteside psychiatric injury?
If so, was the resulting stress caused by any, and if so, what breaches of contract by LBC?
If so, could the resulting psychiatric injury have been avoided by LBC taking appropriate and reasonable steps to avoid those breaches?

The Court concluded in relation to risk assessments:-

63. The PTD had in place detailed Health and Safety policies which were coupled with a policy of undertaking regular risk assessments of the working environment and, where appropriate of the risk of work-related illness arising for particularly vulnerable employees from the working environment. These policies were extended to the identific-ation and elimination or amelioration of stressful working conditions. Departmental risk assessments were undertaken within the UDD on two occasions in the period with which I am concerned. The procedure was for the Departmental Safety Advisor to prepare a stress and General Office risk assessment and for these to be considered and, if necessary adapted, in discussion with the employees affected by those particular assessments. The intention was that risks would be identified and the risk factors giving rise to any appreciable risk would then be reduced or eliminated. The policy of undertaking risk assessments was introduced in 2002 and the UDD was provided with risk assessments in September 2002 and March 2003. The relevant assessment, that of stress, yielded a low/medium assessment following the first assessment and a medium assessment following the second.

64. The following risk factors were being assessed:

"Nervous break downs, depression, low morale, low self esteem, poor concentration, panic attacks, lack of control, irritability, nausea, headaches, migraines, anxiety, anger, high level of accidents, sickness, and absences, long term illness."
A medium assessed risk, as was provided in March 2003, required additional control measures to be complied with within four weeks.

65. Following the receipt of these assessments, Mr Whiteside provided his comments and returned them to Mr Beedham. However, nothing further was done either to check the assessment or to identify and work towards the eradication of the identified risk factors. Given the significant incidence of virtually all of these risk factors amongst most members of the UDD, urgent steps should have been taken to improve the health and to reduce the risk of health breakdown within that department. Furthermore, Regulation 3 of the Health and Safety at Work Regulations (1999) requires employers to assess the risks to workers and any others affected by the undertaking and to record any significant findings. However, nothing was done, certainly in Mr Whiteside's remaining time in the department.

66. Allied to these general risk assessments were, or should have been, specific risk assessments of Mr Whiteside. Following his breakdown and return to work in 2000, he should have been provided with an occupational health risk assessment on a regular basis of the risk factors associated with his stress levels. LBC had been advised that his psychiatric health was placed at risk by enhanced stress levels which were themselves at risk as a result of organisational problems associated with Mr Whiteside's health. Regrettably, no stress risk assessment was ever carried out for Mr Whiteside.

The Court summarised as to breach of duty:-

(4) Was the resulting stress caused by any, and if so, which breaches of contract by LBC

85. The various management failures that have been identified in this judgment culminating in the complete mishandling of the Pro-logis appeal and Mr Whiteside's role in that appeal are cumulatively and individually clear breaches of LBC's contractual duty to take all reasonable steps to protect the health and safety of Mr Whiteside. The unacceptable stressful conditions that Mr Whiteside was subjected to for at least two years prior to his recurrent illness were all caused by a catalogue of breaches by LBC of this duty.

(5) Could the resulting psychiatric injury have been avoided by LBC taking appropriate and reasonable steps to avoid those breaches

86. Had Mr Whiteside not been subjected to unacceptable stress levels and working conditions over that period of at least two years, the evidence suggests that his risk of a naturally occurring depressive illness would have been significantly reduced. **On a balance of probabilities, he would not have incurred any, or any significant psychiatric illness when he did had LBC taken appropriate and reasonable steps to avoid the breaches.**

CHAPTER TWELVE
THE FUTURE OF EL CLAIMS, FUNDAMENTAL DISHONESTY, QOCS AND SMALL CLAIMS TRACK

The landscape for Employers' Liability Claims has changed dramatically since July 2013. We have been through the portal changes and fixed costs changes, but the MOJ is not prepared to leave matters there. The increase in the small claims track is now proposed for April or October 2017 and it may be argued that this will effectively wipe out low value EL claims, in terms of Lawyers undertaking the work.

This chapter therefore seeks to examine the recent and upcoming changes in relation to EL claims.

Fundamental Dishonesty

Claimant Practitioners are now finding more commonly that insurers are alleging fundamental dishonesty, for example where the Claimant's version of events, differs to that reported to the insurer by the policy-holder/employer. Employer's Liability practitioners therefore need to be aware of the rules surrounding fundamental dishonesty and QOCS.

The section was implemented by section 57 of the *Criminal Courts and Justice Act 2015* which sets out:-

> *Personal injury claims: cases of fundamental dishonesty*
> *(1) This section applies where, in proceedings on a claim for damages in respect of personal injury ("the primary claim")—*
> *(a) the court finds that the claimant is entitled to damages in respect of the claim, but*
> *(b) on an application by the defendant for the dismissal of the claim under this section, the court is satisfied on the balance of probabilities that the claimant has been fundamentally dishonest in relation to the primary claim or a related claim.*

(2) The court must dismiss the primary claim, unless it is satisfied that the claimant would suffer substantial injustice if the claim were dismissed.

(3) The duty under subsection (2) includes the dismissal of any element of the primary claim in respect of which the claimant has not been dishonest.

(4) The court's order dismissing the claim must record the amount of damages that the court would have awarded to the claimant in respect of the primary claim but for the dismissal of the claim.

(5) When assessing costs in the proceedings, a court which dismisses a claim under this section must deduct the amount recorded in accordance with subsection (4) from the amount which it would otherwise order the claimant to pay in respect of costs incurred by the defendant.

(6) If a claim is dismissed under this section, subsection (7) applies to

—

(a) any subsequent criminal proceedings against the claimant in respect of the fundamental dishonesty mentioned in subsection (1)(b), and

(b) any subsequent proceedings for contempt of court against the claimant in respect of that dishonesty.

(7) If the court in those proceedings finds the claimant guilty of an offence or of contempt of court, it must have regard to the dismissal of the primary claim under this section when sentencing the claimant or otherwise disposing of the proceedings.

(8) In this section—

"claim" includes a counter-claim and, accordingly, "claimant" includes a counter-claimant and "defendant" includes a defendant to a counter-claim;

"personal injury" includes any disease and any other impairment of a person's physical or mental condition;

"related claim" means a claim for damages in respect of personal injury which is made— (a)in connection with the same incident or series of incidents in connection with which the primary claim is made, and (b)by a person other than the person who made the primary claim.

(9) This section does not apply to proceedings started by the issue of a claim form before the day on which this section comes into force.

One can note with interest how the section is now being used by insurers in respect of low value injury cases. Whereas previously an insurer would have been required to plead fraud, in respect of such cases, the same is no longer true for cases issued after April 2015. It is a common misconception that fundamental dishonesty under section 57 needs to be pleaded, it does not. Insurers are free to turn up at Trial, see how the evidence comes out, and if the Claimant has lied under oath or has exaggerated a claim in some way, make submissions concerning fundamental dishonesty, to dismiss the claim and seek costs. Some insurers are also choosing to plead that a claim has been fundamentally dishonest from the outset.

There has been much debate as to what *'fundamental dishonesty'* means and one of the first reported cases that has looked at the issue can be found in *Creech v Apple Security Group Limited, Severn Valley Railway (Holdings) Ltd and Irvin Leisure Entertainments Limited (unreported) Telford CC 25 March 2015*. District Judge Rogers set out:

> *"Having heard the oral evidence of the claimant and the defendants' witnesses, I have reached, as I explained in my judgment, the very clear view that this accident could not have and did not occur in anything like the circumstances suggested by the claimant. Although I shy away in semantic terms in normal circumstances from the use of the word 'dishonest', in the context of the rules in this case I am quite unable to find anything other than this is a case where the case advanced by the claimant must, to his knowledge, have been incorrect. He must know that he could not, once my findings were made, have been right. This accident did not occur as he said it did, and he must have known that. In my judgment, that advancing of a case so plainly against the weight of the evidence, in the circumstances that I have outlined, can only be described as a fundamentally dishonest claim, and whilst it gives me no pleasure to say so, I am satisfied in the context of this case that qualified one-way costs shifting should not apply, and the second defendant is entitled to his costs as against the claimant".*

Against this context, it is extremely important that practitioners check and double check, with the Claimant that the Claims Notification

Form (CNF), Particulars of Claim, Schedule of Loss and any Part 18 Responses, are correct (i.e. in accordance with the Claimant's instructions) before they are filed and served. The CNF arguably, can be the most fatal document in a whole case, and one must bear in mind what the protocol says about this:-

> *"6.6 The statement of truth in the CNF must be signed either by the claimant or by the claimant's legal representative where the claimant has authorised the legal representative to do so and **the legal representative can produce written evidence of that authorisation**. Where the claimant is a child the statement of truth may be signed by the parent or guardian. On the electronically completed CNF the person may enter their name in the signature box to satisfy this requirement"*

It is therefore essential that the Claimant has seen the CNF before it is submitted to the Portal and approved it and approval is not just sought on the telephone. The Claimant Solicitor's client care letter should contain a warning about fundamental dishonesty and the consequences of such a finding i.e QOCS will be dis-applied, the Claimant will end up paying the Defendant's costs and perhaps being added to the insurance fraud register.

It may also be extremely important for practitioners to:-

a) Check and re-check CNF forms before they are issued to ensure they are accurate and reflect the Claimant's instructions.

b) Check and re-check the medical report with the Claimant, before it is disclosed to ensure that it is factually correct accordingly to the Claimant's instructions.

c) Ensure the pleadings, witness statement, Reply to Defence and any Part 18 responses, are 100% correct and reflect the Claimant's evidence/instructions.

d) If the Claimant's first language is not English, ensure that all documents with statements of truth, including the CNF and the medical report are translated into the Claimant's own language and the documents are taken in the Claimant's own language.

e) Pay particular attention to the schedule of loss to ensure it is 100% accurate, not over stated and is reflective of the claimant's instructions.

Defendants and insurers, will now it may be argued, seek to use section 57 to dismiss genuine claims where minor parts of the claims have been overstated, sometimes by mistake either by the Claimant or Solicitor. A common example may be physiotherapy, pleaded with a statement of truth, claimed where the Claimant has recovered, and the treatment was not undertaken. This, it may be argued, will be fundamentally dishonest. A further example may be a Claimant who says in a statement "*I recovered in accordance with the prognosis in the medical report*", yet say in the witness box, he recovered much earlier, again this is an over statement of his injury and arguably dishonest.

The answer will be to check, check, and re-check with the Claimant any document with a statement of truth and all special damages documents before they are filed/served to make sure it is 100% correct. Claimants may no longer be given the benefit of the doubt in the witness box for such mistakes.

Time needs to be taken particularly with Claimants whose first language is not English, and warnings given at the outset of all cases as to the consequences of section 57. The most common problem area at Trial is medical reports and Claimants who do not read them before they are served i.e. previous accident/injuries, attendance at GP/Hospital, time off work, injuries sustained etc. It is now more important than ever, that with section 57, these are checked in detail with the Claimant before the report is disclosed and if it is wrong, the report be amended, subject to the medical expert confirming the amendment. A failure to do so, may be fatal.

Fundamental dishonesty is arguably a key tool for insurers in fighting fraud in false claims, but Claimant Lawyers must make sure it is not abused by the use of the Act to dismiss claims for minor inconsistencies. It remains to be seen how the Act will be interpreted by the Courts.

QOCS: A Warning: CPR 44.16

This sets out:-

> Exceptions to qualified one-way costs shifting where permission required
> *44.16*
>
> *(1) Orders for costs made against the claimant may be enforced to the full extent of such orders with the permission of the court where the claim is found on the balance of probabilities to be fundamentally dishonest.*
> *(2) Orders for costs made against the claimant may be enforced up to the full extent of such orders with the permission of the court, and to the extent that it considers just, where –*
> *(a) the proceedings include a claim which is made for the financial benefit of a person other than the claimant or a dependant within the meaning of section 1(3) of the Fatal Accidents Act 1976 (other than a claim in respect of the gratuitous provision of care, earnings paid by an employer or medical expenses); or*
> *(b) a claim is made for the benefit of the claimant other than a claim to which this Section applies.*
> *(3) Where paragraph (2)(a) applies, the court may, subject to rule 46.2, make an order for costs against a person, other than the claimant, for whose financial benefit the whole or part of the claim was made.*

A number of well known insurers have openly set out in the press the number of findings achieved under CPR 44.16. In the *Creech* case DJ Rogers stated:-

"There is, however, an exception to that if the court is satisfied that in relation to the claimant's case there has been fundamental dishonesty on the claimant's part. The problem is that there is absolutely no decided authority, or reported case, on what is meant by the phrase 'fundamental dishonesty'. It may be of course that that is because those matters cause difficulty very rarely, if at all. It may be that it is felt

that a decision at first instance, once reached, is so self-evidently unchallengeable

that there is no recourse to appeal to the High Court or the Court of Appeal. There is an unreported case of His Honour Judge Maloney in Cambridge County Court on entirely different facts than those presented before me in this case. In that case, the defendant was able to show that the claimant, having been confronted with evidence as to how he might have suffered a fall from a ladder, changed his account of how he had come to do that and, furthermore, having done that in relation to liability, plainly deceived, or attempted to deceive as to the extent of his injuries, such deception being uncovered by video surveillance evidence used by the defendants. It is unsurprising in that case that His Honour Judge Maloney had little difficulty in deciding that there had been fundamental dishonesty on the part of the claimant"

The case of *Gosling* was the case referred to in *Creech*. Another example can be found in *Zimi v London Central Bus Company 2015 (unreported)* HHJ Madge said:-

" Clearly, the adjective 'fundamental' is important in considering whether or not there has been a claim which is fundamentally dishonest. I assume that the word, fundamental, means something going to the base, something going to the core of the claim, something of central importance and something which is crucial.

A few minutes ago, I gave a detailed judgment on questions of liability. I am not going to repeat now what I said in that judgment in any detail. I came to the conclusion that I was not satisfied that there was a collision, but that if there was it had occurred while the defendant's bus was stationary. Whilst perhaps out of charity to the claimant, I did not specifically find in my judgment that his evidence was fundamentally dishonest, I did refer to a number of issues of credibility. I am satisfied that this is not a claim which could have been brought in a mistaken belief. The claimant cannot have had an honest belief that there was a collision of the kind claimed. This is not a case in which there is any question of the claimant being naïve or unworldly. I bear in mind the previous claims of a similar nature, which he has made.

Having regard to the matters to which I referred in my judgment and to the matters to which I have just referred to I am satisfied that the claimant's claim was fundamentally dishonest".

It may be argued that QOCS is being used in numerous ways for the Defendant to recover its costs and in must be borne in mind that this does not only apply to cases of fundamental dishonesty, but it can also can apply to other scenarios as follows:-

Exceptions to qualified one-way costs shifting where permission not required

44.15 Orders for costs made against the claimant may be enforced to the full extent of such orders without the permission of the court where the proceedings have been struck out on the grounds that –

(a) the claimant has disclosed no reasonable grounds for bringing the proceedings;
(b) the proceedings are an abuse of the court's process; or
(c) the conduct of –
(i) the claimant; or
(ii) a person acting on the claimant's behalf and with the claimant's knowledge of such conduct, is likely to obstruct the just disposal of the proceedings.

The Claimant therefore cannot issue proceedings for cases with no merits or credibility concerns, discontinue and rely upon QOCS protection. It is open to the Defendant to seek to aside the Notice of

Discontinuance, and ask for the claim be struck out under CPR 44.15 or ask the Court to make a finding that it is fundamentally dishonest under CPR 44.16. There are now examples where insurers are taking this course of action. Once upon a time the insurer may have been happy to take the saving of the success fee/ATE premium of pre April 2013 cases, but those days seem to be behind us, in such cases.

Conclusions and the Small Claims Track

George Osbourne announced in October 2015 that the small claims track would be increased to £5,000. This has caused fury amongst Personal Injury Lawyers and again raised significant arguments over Access to Justice. All the signs now point to an implementation date of April or October 2017. It remains to be seen whether the limit will actually be increased to £5,000, whether it will include only RTA claims or all EL/PL claims and more details will be provided following a consultation in early 2016.

What is certain is that the changes, however they fall, are going to present serious problems for Personal Injury practitioners in maintaining a stable business model. It may be argued that those who practice EL claims will be more insulated as generally speaking EL claims tend to have more significant injuries and often tend to be more complicated than RTA cases, which means they are less likely to be small claims.

One has serious doubts as to whether a Litigant in Person, could litigate even a basic EL case. The issues and law are often more complex, the pleadings are difficult to draft and the factual and causation issues can also be complicated. Undoubtedly, post 2017, there will still be a requirement for Personal Injury Lawyers in this type of work, but the role of the Personal Injury Lawyer is likely to have to evolved and it may well be that we see the introduction of Contingency Fee arrangements, in a revised format in this area of work.

Lightning Source UK Ltd.
Milton Keynes UK
UKOW06f0317240516

274876UK00001B/78/P